Developmental Education in an Era of High Standards

Jim Grant

MODERN LEARNING PRESS
ROSEMONT, NJ

ISBN 1-56762-094-9

Developmental Education
in an Era of High Standards

Printed in the United States of America. All rights reserved. For more information, contact Modern Learning Press, P.O. Box 167, Rosemont, NJ 08556.

Item #520

To Jay LaRoche,
for his outstanding management as President
of the Society For Developmental Education,
which gave me the freedom I needed
to make this book a reality.

A very special thank you
to Robert Low,
for his guidance, insight and patience during
his editing and collaboration in writing this book,
and for his moral courage and
willingness to take on a manuscript
that challenges the conventional wisdom
about educational reform.

Contents

Introduction

"Let's create standards that are so high most young children won't be able to reach them. That way, the students will have to keep working really hard no matter how smart they are and how well they're really doing."

"Let's link these overly high standards to standardized tests that don't measure what is actually taught in the classroom. Then, we can pick one single point score as the basis for meeting the standards, and any child who gets even one point less will have failed to meet the standards."

"To show that we're really getting tough with these kids, let's automatically flunk every child who scores even one point too low on the test, making them spend another year in the same grade with younger children. It may not teach them anything, but we have to threaten them with something so they'll stay motivated to learn."

"And just to make sure everyone knows we really mean business, we won't allow any exceptions for any reason. And we certainly won't let an understanding of child development, the concerns of parents and teachers, the tremendous expense of these plans, and the fact that they have never been proven to work stop us from doing exactly what we want."

If statements like these sound outrageous to you, you are not alone. Parents and educators across America are responding with growing alarm as the movement to establish high standards is being taken to illogical and destructive extremes by individuals who are driven by ideology and personal gain, rather than by the needs of our children. And what is truly outrageous is that policies like those described in the preceding paragraphs are actually being inflicted on American children.

Consider the following:

- A 1998 article in *The American School Board Journal* warned school boards about the standards developed for the state of Virginia, because those standards were so far out of sync with young children's capabilities and needs.

- A 1998 article in *Education Week* reported that parents were suing a Texas school district, because their children were being forced to repeat a grade on the basis of a single score on a standardized test that had not been developed for the purpose of evaluating a child's ability to proceed to the next grade level.

- Meanwhile, as various politicians and education bureaucrats rushed to jump on the runaway standards bandwagon, *no* article in *any* publication I was aware of was reporting *any* clear and convincing research showing that *any* of these policies were providing *any* benefits at *any* actual schools.

Is this any way to improve the performance of America's students and schools? Of course not. It's simply a continuation of the same destructive pattern of extreme and ill-considered "reforms" that have been plaguing America's schools and hurting America's children for far too long. And now, more than ever, there is an urgent need for concerned, responsible parents and educators both to protect and improve their schools.

The good news is that we can accomplish this, by using a common-sense approach to establishing standards that are based on children's developmental and individual capabilities and needs. That's why I prepared this revised edition of a book I previously wrote when America's schools and children were being endangered by the previous round of failed attempts at school reform. A brief look back at that experience provides a much-needed perspective on what's happening now, as well as what we need to do about it.

The previous edition of this book was entitled *Developmental Education in the 1990s*, and it was written to protect children and schools from overly zealous proponents of "developmentally appropriate practices." Among other things, these extremists claimed that teaching young children skills and correct spelling was bad for the children, and that providing some young children with an additional year of time to learn and grow was bad for those children, and that all the young children in America were going to "catch up" with each other in third grade, at which point they would all be able to learn and do what they needed to succeed in school.

As ridiculous as this all sounds now, the fact of the matter is that in the early 1990s the "ayatollahs of appropriate education" were loudly denouncing many well-established and effective educational practices, and many teachers were *forced* to adopt a version of "developmentally appropriate practices" they could not believe in and that did not work, on orders from some state department of education bureaucrats and local administrators who believed in—or were simply intimidated by—the supposed reformers.

As predicted in my book and others—and as anyone with common sense and first-hand experience with children might expect—depriving students of needed skills and learning time did not enable them to catch up with each other. Instead, it resulted in large numbers of children failing to be able learn and work successfully in the upper grades, and then having to be "socially promoted" to the next grade, where they remained unable to learn and work successfully because they had fallen so far behind.

This combination of skills deprivation and social promotion led to a total lack of standards in some schools, so the natural and logical reaction was to re-establish standards that would require schools to teach skills and prepare students in the same grade to successfully learn the same material at the same time. So far, so good.

Then, unfortunately, this reasonable reaction was taken too far in the opposite direction by similar sorts of extremists and opportunists, who once again were more focused on their own personal or political agendas than on the real needs of our children and our schools. So, instead of delaying skills instruction too long, now some educators are being *forced* to provide too much skills instruction too soon. And instead of preventing any children from receiving an additional year to learn and grow in school, some educators are now being *forced* to retain any child for a whole year because the child had a one-point score deficiency on an inappropriate standardized test.

I don't know about you, but I'm *not* just going to sit back and watch as America's students and schools get victimized once again in the name of "education reform." I've written this book and now I'm going on the road to work with principals, teachers, and parents across America, in order to help develop a responsible and effective approach to education and standards that will stop these wild and harmful "pendulum swings" from hurting our students and our schools.

Moral outrage is not enough. We need to take effective action now—at the local level as well as nationally. So, if you'd like to be part of this vital and positive process, take a look through the questions and answers that appear on the following pages. And be sure to note that if you purchased this book and want to share a page of information with educators or parents at your school, we're giving you the right to photocopy that page and pass it on to them. That's how committed we are to getting the word out, and I hope you share the spirit and the information, for the sake of all our children and our schools.

Developmental Education in an Era of High Standards

Q. What is developmental education?

A. Developmental education is an approach to teaching that matches the curriculum and methods of instruction to a child's current stage of development and individual needs.

This approach recognizes that young children pass through a series of developmental stages as they mature, and that the teaching methods and materials appropriate for older students may actually prevent slightly younger children from learning. For example, a kindergarten student who does not yet understand abstract symbols—such as the numeral 3 or the word *three*—may still be able to count three blocks or other objects. This child can successfully learn and work with "hands-on" classroom materials, which should be combined with exposure to numbers and words. However, this same child is likely to "fail" if expected to learn by completing a workbook that contains only numbers and words.

While virtually all children pass through the same series of stages, the age and rate at which they do so vary. Children who are as much as a year ahead or a year behind other children born on the same day may still be considered within a normal range of development. Moreover, the rate at which children may pass through a stage or move from one stage to the next can also vary, as some children simply need more time to learn and grow than others, even though they are equally intelligent. That's why developmental education takes into consideration the child's *developmental age*—the child's current stage of development—as well as the child's chronological age.

This developmental approach also recognizes the importance of nurturing four key areas of a child's development—intellectual, emotional, social, and physical (including neurological)—because they are inter-related and can all have a profound effect on a child's learning. Physiological limitations, emotional upsets, and social problems can all interfere with a child's ability to absorb information and do school work. A developmental approach therefore supports all aspects of a child's development, rather than focusing exclusively on intellectual growth.

In these and other ways, developmental education is child-compatible because it recognizes that the most effective learning occurs when each child's unique needs and capabilities are understood and respected.

Q. What are the developmental stages young students pass through?

A. The development of young children is a complex process, and children's stages of development can be defined in a number of different ways. These differing perspectives are not necessarily contradictory; they simply emphasize different aspects of the developmental process.

To cite one influential example, Jean Piaget, the eminent Swiss psychologist, found that children's thought processes evolve through a series of stages. Preschool and kindergarten students are usually in what Piaget called the *pre-operational* stage, in which the children are still developing the capacity to use language and understand the relationship between words and objects. At about age 6 or 7, children enter the *concrete operations* stage, during which they become fully capable of mentally manipulating symbols such as words and numbers.

Arnold Gesell, the founding father of developmental education, found that specific stages of emotional and social development were also associated with children's ages. He noted that 5-year-olds tended to be calm, happy, and eager to please, but from 5 ½ to 6 ½ children often go through a "break-up" stage in which they are more egocentric, rebellious, and emotional. Then, at age 7, the same children are likely to be more withdrawn and solitary. Gesell and his colleagues also identified changes and patterns in children's physical development, finding, for example, that the ability to sit still and focus attention develops gradually, making extended "seat work" for 4- and 5-year-olds much more difficult than it usually is for older students.

Educators have also found that children pass through a series of stages in learning to read and write. Beginning readers usually need to work on memorizing sight words and sounding out letters before they can master sound/symbol correspondence and focus on comprehending complex text. Beginning writers tend to find that the basic strokes required for printed handwriting are much easier than the more complex strokes and joinings required for writing in script, which is why the transition to script usually occurs toward the end of second grade or in third grade.

Developmental education has proven to be successful because it links the curriculum and methods of instruction to an understanding of these varying developmental patterns. This approach enables educators to make full use of children's interest and time in school, creating an ongoing series of successful learning experiences, rather than wasting precious time and creating a pattern of failure by pressuring students to learn and perform in ways that exceed their current capabilities.

Q. How has developmental education traditionally worked in American schools?

A. Developmental education has enabled generations of American students to achieve success in school by preventing children from being placed in the wrong grade or program, providing them with an appropriate curriculum, and offering time-flexibility options when students need additional learning time.

Knowing that some students were developing at a slower but still normal rate compared to their chronological peers, developmental educators have long considered many other factors in addition to birthdates when making initial grade placement decisions. This is particularly important for *late bloomers*—children of average or above intelligence who tend to do very well in school when given adequate time to mature, but who often develop patterns of frustration and failure when placed in a grade for which they are not yet ready. The first years of school usually set the tone for the years that follow, so developmental educators carefully considered young children's readiness to succeed in school and offered alternatives that matched children's differing stages of development.

During the 1970s and 1980s in particular, many schools offered *pre-kindergarten* classes for children who were at the legal chronological age to start school but who were not yet ready to learn and work successfully in a typical kindergarten class. Also available at many schools were *transition* classes, which provided an additional year to learn and grow in a new classroom when students were not yet ready to switch to the more academically rigorous environment of first grade. Still other students were allowed to continue learning in the same classroom with the same teacher—the educational process known as grade-level *retention*.

Providing an additional year of learning time was found to be far more effective at the start of students' schooling than in later years, when a pattern of frustration and failure had already been established, and when students were often far more sensitive about changing to a different grade level. And whether or not students received an additional year of learning time, developmental educators tried to make sure the curriculum and methods of instruction matched the students' differing developmental needs and capabilities. The variety of options available allowed this to happen without "dumbing down" a grade-level curriculum to the level of the least ready students, or having them struggle and fail in a grade geared to more advanced students.

By combining an appropriate curriculum with time-flexibility options, schools that used a developmental approach were truly ready for their students and could accommodate a wide range of developmental differences successfully.

From *Developmental Education in an Era of High Standards* by Jim Grant. Published by Modern Learning Press, Inc., P.O. Box 167, Rosemont, NJ 08556, 1-800-627-5867. This page may be reproduced by the individual purchaser only for his or her own use.

Q. Is the developmental approach still right for today's students?

A. Yes. Developmental education is even more important for today's diverse student population, because so many more students are not coming to school well prepared to achieve success.

Today's classrooms are far more likely than those of previous decades to include students who come from dysfunctional and/or impoverished families, students who have not received adequate pre-natal or post-natal health care, students who speak English as a second language, students who have been exposed prematurely to illegal drugs or environmental hazards, and students who have been identified as having a learning disability or other special needs. These sorts of factors and circumstances clearly prevent many students from learning as quickly and effectively as other students who have not experienced these types of problems. And while time-flexibility options should not be used as a substitute for other interventions specifically designed to alleviate these factors and circumstances, the reality is that these factors and circumstances often result in students needing additional learning time to master the grade-level material that their problems have prevented them from learning.

Moreover, an increasing number of students suffer not just from one of the problematic factors and circumstances listed above, but from "multiple, co-occurring factors and circumstances" that interfere with their ability to succeed in school. Meanwhile, the percentage of late bloomers in any grade has remained relatively constant over the past few decades, because patterns of development often re-occur within families—as grown-up late bloomers beget little late bloomers of their own. And, of course, late bloomers are just as likely as other children to suffer from the other sorts of factors and circumstances described above, which make them even more in need of alternatives that provide additional learning time.

For all these reasons, the range of developmental and individual differences now found in many classrooms is even greater than it was in the past, and this creates an even greater need to match the curriculum and methods of instruction to students' current needs and capabilities, as well as to provide additional learning time for those students who need it. Essentially, developmental education works beautifully now, because it is an inclusive approach designed to accommodate children learning at different levels, by providing a curriculum and time-flexibility options that match their needs, and thereby enabling them to achieve school success.

From *Developmental Education in an Era of High Standards* by Jim Grant. Published by Modern Learning Press, Inc., P.O. Box 167, Rosemont, NJ 08556, 1-800-627-5867. This page may be reproduced by the individual purchaser only for his or her own use.

Q. How well do the developmental stages and needs of today's students correspond to the grade-level standards now being created for many schools?

A. When standards take into account the variability of students' development and needs, they can become effective and meaningful guideposts that improve the performance of students and their schools. However, when standards are derived from texts and tests, rather than the actual capabilities of today's students, the inevitable result is the failure of many students, as well as the failure of the standards to improve our schools.

Knowing that children's stages and rates of development vary widely, and that this developmental diversity is often compounded by a wide variety of other factors and circumstances that can have a negative impact on students' learning, the creators of effective standards establish realistic goals and recognize that some children will need more time to reach the goals. This does *not* mean those children are "failures;" it simply means that more learning time and appropriate instruction are needed by some students, which is a reasonable expectation for meaningful standards in today's educational environment.

Unfortunately, some standards are based on unrealistic expectations for the sort of *non-standardized* student population now found in most American schools. These sorts of standards pressure many children to try to learn and perform in ways that are not yet right for them, making them less likely to do well in school and more likely to have negative attitudes about school and themselves.

In addition, some standards are being linked to the achievement of a specific score on a standardized test, even though many young students are not good at taking such tests. This sort of standard increases the pressure on educators to "teach to the test" by drilling students on test-taking skills and the particular types of information included on the tests, rather than using the types of methods and materials that are actually best suited to the education of the students. The negative consequences of this approach also tend to spread downward through the grades, increasing the pressure on lower-grade teachers to help prepare students for what they will encounter in the grades ahead, rather than focusing on students' current needs and capabilities.

As with so many other aspects of education, when standards are truly child-compatible they can contribute to school success, but standards that are driven by ideology and statistical manipulation are likely to victimize many students—and ultimately become just one more failed attempt at school reform.

Q. How does developmental education help students meet the grade-level standards being set for them?

A. A developmental approach helps students learn efficiently, and it provides the time-flexibility options some children need in order to meet grade-level standards.

Students are far more likely to learn more—and learn more quickly—when the instructional methods and materials being used match their current needs and developmental stages. By presenting information in ways that are interesting and fully comprehensible, developmental educators make the best possible use of valuable instructional time and stimulate enthusiasm for learning. This approach provides students with the solid foundation of knowledge and positive attitudes that lead to continued success in the upper grades.

Developmental education also enables children who need additional learning time to obtain it when it will do the most good—right at the start of their school careers. Rather than allowing children to struggle and fail for years and then finally "flunk" when they are old enough to deeply resent it, developmental educators can make an additional year of learning time an effective, continuous-progress experience, which sustains and contributes to a pattern of success and interest in learning.

This is especially important now that some grade-level standards are being linked to automatic retention policies, which mandate another year in the same grade for students who do not achieve a specified score on a standardized test. An additional year of learning time is far more likely to be effective when it is spent in a supportive environment at the start of a student's school career. This approach prevents intelligent, hard-working students who are developing more slowly from being victimized by a harsh and rigid system, which may initially place them in an *inappropriate* grade and then demand that they do just as well as other students who are far more advanced or have other advantages.

The linking of standards to automatic retention policies has already led some leading educators to call for the introduction of transition classes in the upper grades, as well as in the lower grades, to avoid the wholesale flunking of large numbers of students who did not receive the additional learning time they needed earlier in their school careers. In ways such as this, the developmental approach provides the combination of appropriate curriculum and time-flexibility that is a vital part of the implementation of effective standards in our schools.

School Readiness
in an Era of
High Standards

Q. What is school readiness?

A. Essentially, school readiness refers to the fit between a beginning student and the particular grade or class in which the child will be placed. When the child and the grade or class are a good match for each other, the child is very likely to learn well and enjoy school. But when children find themselves in a grade or class for which they are not yet ready, the children are likely to experience frustration and failure, and then develop negative attitudes about school and themselves.

This experience is known as *wrong grade placement*, and in order for it to be prevented, the children and the school have to be ready for each other. The children need to have a solid physical, social, emotional, and intellectual foundation so that they are prepared to learn successfully. And the school needs to have options available to accommodate a diverse range of incoming students, including some who are developing more slowly and others whose readiness has been affected by other factors and circumstances.

For example, some children who are developing more slowly—or are simply the very youngest children in a grade—become outstanding students in kindergarten and the upper grades if given an additional year of growing and learning time before or after starting kindergarten. Other developmentally or chronologically young students who go right into kindergarten and then first grade fall behind and may be unable to learn well and meet grade-level standards, simply because they were not yet ready to succeed in the grades in which they were initially placed. There are also children who are *not* developmentally young but still need additional learning time to overcome the effects of dysfunctional family situations, poverty, medical problems, severely traumatic experiences, limited English proficiency, or other factors that can affect school readiness.

To be ready for students who have these sorts of needs, schools need a diverse range of educational programs, including readiness and transition classes that provide an additional year of continuous-progress learning in a supportive educational environment. This is especially important now that many schools are setting high standards, which many students are not yet ready to meet and which may therefore result in even more students experiencing frustration and failure in school.

From *Developmental Education in an Era of High Standards* by Jim Grant. Published by Modern Learning Press, Inc., P.O. Box 167, Rosemont, NJ 08556, 1-800-627-5867. This page may be reproduced by the individual purchaser only for his or her own use.

11

Q. What are the most important aspects of a child's readiness for school?

A. Readiness for school encompasses the physical, social/emotional, and intellectual realms, just as a child's overall development does. Obviously, there is a lot of overlap among these areas, and when they are working well together they can help propel a child to success. On the other hand, when one or more of these areas are interfering with others, they can prevent a child from achieving school success.

Important physical capabilities include the accurate vision and hearing that enable children to absorb information, and the motor skills that enable children to draw, write, and work with hands-on objects. Recent research on the brain has also confirmed that the growth and development of the brain can have a profound effect on children's ability to learn.

In the social/emotional area, young children should be able to separate from their parents or guardians and then start learning comfortably with educators and fellow classmates. They need to be able to work through the inevitable upsets and conflicts that occur in a group setting, and hopefully they will not be experiencing serious emotional problems outside of school that distract them from learning.

Intellectually, young children should know basic information about themselves and other family members, such as names, ages, where they live, and so forth. Children should also have some familiarity with the alphabet, single-digit numbers, and the names of colors and common household objects.

Children who have all these characteristics are well prepared for the methods and materials typically used in today's kindergartens. While these characteristics are not rigid requirements, and today's educators need to be prepared to work effectively with young children who lack some or even many of them, it must also be understood that time spent helping some children learn basic information and skills leaves less time for these children to learn the grade-level material on which high standards are based.

Q. How should educators evaluate the readiness of new students?

A. Information from a variety of sources can and should be used to evaluate the readiness of an incoming student. Rather than relying on a single source of information, educators have a responsibility to compile different types of information in their effort to gain an understanding of the "whole child."

Some educators use a developmental assessment or readiness screening device to evaluate the child's current developmental level or overall school readiness. These "instruments" provide a score or other measurement based on the child's performance of simple, age-appropriate tasks, such as completing a drawing of a person or identifying some common objects.

Educators can also use an observational checklist to compile information about a child during an initial visit to a kindergarten classroom—or even during the first weeks of school. In addition, educators and parents working together can complete a checklist or questionnaire that compiles important background information about the child's family, health, previous experiences, and other factors or circumstances that can affect a child's readiness for school. Information from preschool teachers and caregivers can also provide valuable insights about the child's capabilities, as well as any unique needs.

Because readiness refers to the fit between the child and the school, information of this sort should always be considered along with information about the grade-level curriculum appropriate for the child, as well as any alternatives that may be available. Only then do educators and parents have the full range of information needed to make decisions that are truly in the child's best interests.

From *Developmental Education in an Era of High Standards* by Jim Grant. Published by Modern Learning Press, Inc., P.O. Box 167, Rosemont, NJ 08556, 1-800-627-5867. This page may be reproduced by the individual purchaser only for his or her own use.

13

Q. How should educators and parents use information about school readiness?

A. School readiness information can and should be used in a number of important ways. First and foremost, this information should be used to assign children to the appropriate grade or class—the one in which a child is ready to succeed. As part of this process, information about school readiness should be used to identify children who are likely to benefit from an additional year of learning and growing time.

Parental input should be an integral part of the process of making decisions about school readiness. If educators recommend that a child be placed in a program that provides additional learning time, they need to discuss this recommendation with the parents and solicit additional input from them. The parents may also want to obtain other information and advice—especially from parents of children who received similar recommendations in the past.

Information from other sources such as books and articles can be very helpful, but firsthand knowledge of the particular child and school should always be given the top priority. Parents should be especially wary of statistical analyses which purport to show that additional learning time does not help children. Some studies of this sort have been manipulated for ideological reasons and ignore valid research documenting the value of additional learning time. Most of all, extensive studies covering many schools cannot and do not take into account the specific circumstances of the individual child under consideration.

Parents should be allowed to make the final decision regarding the placement of their child, based on all the information about the child and the options available at the school. Once this decision has been made, educators can then use the same readiness information for curriculum planning purposes. This information can identify what a child already knows and what needs to be taught, as well as the instructional methods and materials most likely to prove effective. In this way, school readiness information can make a vital contribution to school success under any circumstances.

Q.

Why not just base all placement decisions on the state-mandated cut-off dates for school entrance?

A.

There are a number of problems with this overly simplistic and narrow approach, which does *not* take into account many important factors that can influence an individual child's readiness for school.

First and foremost, the use of a single, arbitrary date results in some children struggling and failing in grades for which they were not yet ready, while other children who could succeed are prevented from starting school when they should. For example, in a state where the cut-off date is September 1st, a boy born on August 31st who is developmentally young and affected by other factors that make him even less ready to succeed may still be required to start school, while a girl who was born two days later, is developmentally ready, and is not affected by any negative factors may be *prevented* from starting school even though she would be in the right grade at that time.

Another problem with this approach is the variability of the cut-off dates from state to state. Some states require a child to turn 5 years old during the summer before starting kindergarten, while other states place 4-year-olds in kindergarten if the children will turn 5 before the end of December. These differing cut-off dates are *not* linked to a particularly easy or difficult curriculum. And schools in states that allow 4-year-olds to start kindergarten may have overcrowded classrooms filled with an especially diverse and needy student population, which can make successful learning and teaching all the more difficult.

Allowing the number of candles on a birthday cake to be the sole determinant of a child's readiness for school does a grave disservice to the child and the school. This approach ignores the plentiful evidence showing that children born at about the same time develop at different rates, and that many of today's children have been adversely affected by a variety of other factors and circumstances that make them need additional time to learn and grow, before they can achieve success in school and meet high standards.

From *Developmental Education in an Era of High Standards* by Jim Grant. Published by Modern Learning Press, Inc., P.O. Box 167, Rosemont, NJ 08556, 1-800-627-5867. This page may be reproduced by the individual purchaser only for his or her own use.

15

Q. How does the readiness of today's students compare with that of past generations?

A. During recent decades, there has been a dramatic *decrease* in the number of students who are ready to start school successfully. While the percentage of students who are developing at a slower but still normal rate has remained about the same, many more of today's students have been adversely affected by other factors and circumstances that impede their ability to succeed in school.

Poverty and related conditions have prevented substantial numbers of American children from having the healthy and supportive childhoods they need to succeed. Insufficient health care and nutrition have left many children with physical limitations, while prenatal exposure to tobacco, alcohol, and illegal drugs also interfered with many children's development. In more than a few cases, these circumstances were also combined with dysfunctional home environments and a lack of exposure to books, numbers, and other elements that contribute to school success.

In addition, many affluent children are also less ready to succeed than those of past generations. Affluent children, too, may suffer from prenatal exposure to unhealthy substances or from dysfunctional and unstimulating home environments. And the busy schedules of families in which both parents work have created what some people now call "suburban orphans"—young children who spend very little time with their hard-working parents and do not receive enough emotional or intellectual support from them.

All these children may become stressed, depressed, or angry as a result, and then spend time in the classroom expressing or coping with these feelings. Many of these children—and others—also become overly passive due to excessive amounts of time spent watching television and videos, or playing video and computer games.

In too many cases, day care, preschool, and educational media have not made up for a lack of individual attention in a healthy and stimulating home environment. When young children's basic needs have not been met, they are far less likely to be ready to succeed in school.

Q. How does the lack of readiness correspond with the standards being set for American schools?

A. One teacher spoke for many of her colleagues when she said, "The standards are in one place, and the children are in another."

While the Goals 2000 program was supposed to ensure that all children would start school ready to succeed by the year 2000, studies continue to show that the problems that impede students' ability to learn continue to plague large numbers of American children. Meanwhile, other nations have been far more committed to providing services that enable their children to become successful students.

The poor showing of American students in international competitions has created a desire to establish "world-class standards" for our schools, but there has *not* been a corresponding determination to establish "world-class standards" for our children's health and well-being. The result is an *unlevel* playing field on which too many American students are at a distinct disadvantage. And when these students are expected to meet the same high standards as other students in the U.S. or abroad who do not have similar problems, the students and their schools are set up for failure.

This approach to setting standards is especially detrimental when it is linked to automatic retention and other policies that may further harm children, rather than solving their underlying problems. This is sometimes portrayed as a "get-tough" approach that will force students and their teachers to do better. But while a get-tough approach may be appropriate for criminals, young children who are struggling in school are far more likely to be *victims* of circumstances beyond their control. They need assistance and support that meet their real needs, which may or may not include another year in the same grade.

Effective standards take into account the current readiness of the student population and can then be increased as student readiness and achievement increase. Unfortunately, standards that ignore student readiness are likely to fail students and fail as standards.

Q. What can be done to improve the readiness of American children?

A. The best way to increase children's readiness for school is to start right at the beginning—when children are first developing in the womb.

Appropriate prenatal care, combined with adequate nutrition for pregnant mothers, greatly increases the odds of having healthy babies, who can then continue developing as they should. Of course, proper nutrition and health care must then be provided throughout childhood, so that children are physically capable of succeeding in school and are not distracted from their studies by hunger or worries about having their basic needs met.

Access to high-quality day care and preschool is also vitally important for children whose parents are unable or unwilling to care for them at home in the years prior to kindergarten. And whether or not children are in day care or preschool, their parents should still be reading to them every day and engaging in other activities that support intellectual development in a relaxed and enjoyable way.

Of course, some children will develop at a slower rate even when they receive good health care, proper nutrition, and intellectual stimulation. So, knowing that readiness is the fit between the child and the school, the final step in improving the readiness of American students is for schools to offer a range of options that provide additional learning time, because there will always be some children who are developing more slowly and will therefore need more time to succeed in school and meet high standards.

Developmental Extra-Year Programs in an Era of High Standards

Q. What is the purpose of providing an additional year of learning time during the primary grades?

A. An additional year of learning time is a form of early intervention that enables numerous young children to learn needed skills and achieve school success. This intervention can prevent students from struggling and failing when they are not yet ready for the curriculum and methods of instruction used in a particular grade.

Additional learning time works because young children of the same age do not all develop and grow at the same rate. Even when young children of the same age have reached the same developmental stage, they do not all *learn* at the same rate. In addition, some children lack the basic knowledge and skills on which a grade-level curriculum is based, simply because they have not yet had an opportunity to learn them, so they need additional learning time to master the skills that many other children of the same age already have.

These widespread variations in development, learning rates, and skill levels leave some children unprepared to achieve success in a particular grade or program, until they have had the additional learning and growing time they need. In order to accommodate these types of learners—who are at risk of becoming victims of a rigid, time-bound, lock-step school system—developmental educators have long used extra-year classes to provide students with a "half step" on the way to a new grade or program.

For example, some schools provide *pre-kindergarten* or *readiness* classes for children who are old enough to start school but are not yet ready for the curriculum and methods of instruction used in kindergarten. These same schools and others may also have *transition* classes between kindergarten and first grade—or between other grades. These sorts of classes enable students to move on to a new classroom with a new teacher and a new curriculum that is appropriate for them, rather than being required either to repeat a grade or to be "socially promoted" into a grade in which they are not yet ready to succeed.

Providing an additional year of learning and growing time in a supportive, continuous-progress extra-year class is a positive and preventive approach that meets the needs of many of today's young children. This approach also meets the needs of many educators, who are being required to maintain high grade-level standards rather than "dumbing down" the curriculum to accommodate students who lack the developmental readiness or skills needed to learn grade-level material.

Q. When and how were developmental extra-year classes developed?

A. A few developmental extra-year classes existed as far back as the 1950s. Even then, when many schools had a more relaxed and developmental approach to early childhood education, a significant number of children still needed additional learning and growing time in order to succeed in school.

In the late 1950s, many American schools introduced a more accelerated curriculum in response to fears that the U.S. was falling behind in the "space race" with the Soviet Union. This curriculum became known as the "push-down curriculum," because it was determined by university professors who decided what college freshmen needed to know and used that as the basis for setting standards for each of the lower grades, right down to kindergarten. This top-down approach led to young children being taught more material—and higher-level material—than many of them were capable of handling. And the thoroughly predictable result was that more children began to struggle and fail in school.

In response to these problems, numerous individuals and organizations began focusing attention on the importance of matching the curriculum to the developmental levels of the students—and providing additional learning and growing time for students who were not yet ready to succeed. Beginning in 1966, developmental extra-year classes were established throughout New Hampshire as part of a U.S. Department of Education Title III program. The astute educators who established these classes recognized that academic failures and accompanying bad attitudes in the primary grades often culminated in a decision to drop out of high school many years later. So, developmental extra-time options were introduced as a means of preventing grade-level retention and reducing the high school drop-out rate.

The success of these and other extra-year classes led to the establishment of similar programs throughout America. An additional year of growing and learning time was found to help children from a wide variety of socio-economic levels and regions. By the end of the 1980s, large numbers of developmental extra-year programs could be found in virtually every state.

A number of these programs were abolished in the early 1990s, when a few education organizations tried to prohibit schools from providing *any* students with extra-year classes or grade-level retention. This "forced social promotion" eliminated parent options and choices, and resulted in some schools promoting every student every year, no matter how far behind a student had fallen or how unprepared the student was to succeed in the next grade. The lack of meaningful grade-level standards quickly led to an increase in the number of students who had not mastered basic skills and were therefore unable to learn successfully in the upper grades.

Q. What are the characteristics of a high-quality, developmental program that provides an additional year of learning time in the primary grades?

A. A high-quality extra-year class offers a responsive and challenging educational environment that meets the developmental and academic needs of its students. As a result, the students can learn successfully and enjoyably, which also helps them develop the positive attitudes about school and themselves that contribute to continued success in the upper grades.

The curriculum and methods of instruction accommodate a variety of students and enable them to learn needed information and skills in an appropriate way. Active learning experiences are emphasized, and students' abilities and performance are measured by authentic evaluations and assessments. Students can progress at different rates, and flexible entrance and exit policies are used to prevent students from remaining in the wrong grade or class throughout the year.

High-quality extra-year programs have small class sizes of about 15 to 18 students, so that the teachers have time to provide adequate amounts of individual instruction. There is also an appropriate and diverse mixture of students, so the class does not become a "dumping ground" for students who have severe disabilities or other problems that cannot be solved by an additional year of learning time.

Parents participate in the placement process for the class, providing background information and making the final placement decisions. These decisions are based on children's medical history and their current interests, activities, and capabilities, as well as teachers' observations and data from developmental assessments. Frequent communication between parents, teachers, and supervisors occurs throughout the school year, and parents are welcome as volunteers in the classroom.

Long-term studies follow the progress of participants—as well as other students who were invited to participate but did not do so—to confirm that the classes provide important benefits which are sustained in later years. Input from students, parents, other teachers, and administrators is also considered as part of an ongoing effort to maximize the effectiveness of the classes—and make sure they effectively prepare students to succeed at the next grade level.

The combined effects of all these characteristics make high-quality extra-year classes exemplary models that demonstrate the value of developmental education for all students.

Q. What types of students benefit from an additional year of learning time in a continuous-progress program?

A. There are several types of students who are especially likely to benefit from a continuous-progress extra-year program.

Many "late bloomers"—young children who are developing at a slower but still normal rate—simply need more time to develop before they become capable of doing grade-level work. They are likely to become victims of wrong grade placement and then struggle and fail if schools *only* consider chronological age when making grade placement decisions. An additional year in a supportive educational environment early in their school careers can enable these children to become successful and enthusiastic learners.

Some of the youngest students in a grade are also likely to benefit from an additional year of learning and growing time, because schools' reliance on a single, arbitrary "cut-off" date for entrance and grade placement results in the oldest students in a grade having already had almost a full additional year of growing and learning time. This "head start" gives the older students in a grade a tremendous advantage. And as shown by numerous studies compiled in the book *School Readiness & Transition Programs: Real Facts from Real Schools* by James Uphoff, Ed.D., the youngest students in a grade are far more likely to suffer from a range of school problems, including receiving lower grades, scoring lower on achievement tests, being retained in grade, and even being classified as "learning disabled." These sorts of results show that some of the youngest children in a grade need additional time to learn and grow in order to compete with the older children and succeed in school.

Numerous studies have also shown that young boys tend to develop more slowly than young girls, and that young girls tend to have stronger language and fine-motor skills, which help them do well in the primary grades. A boy who is chronologically or developmentally young is therefore even more likely to be at risk for wrong grade placement and school failure.

Other students likely to benefit from an additional year in a continuous-progress program are those who need time to overcome a deficit of information or experience. Examples might include intelligent children who have been developing at a normal rate but who suffered from a prolonged and serious ailment, or whose family backgrounds deprived them of the basic knowledge and skills on which a primary education is based. An additional year of learning and growing time can enable these students to learn what they need to succeed, rather than allowing their previous deprivation to result in frustration and failure.

Q.

What types of research have been done on continuous-progress extra-year classes?

A.

Numerous research studies have been done on children who participated in developmental extra-year classes, in some cases monitoring their progress right through high school graduation. Parents of the children in the classes have also been surveyed, as have teachers who worked with the children in later grades.

In the book *School Readiness and Transition Classes: Real Facts from Real Schools*, Dr. James Uphoff has compiled more than 35 studies of continuous-progress extra-year programs from across the U.S., some of which served thousands of children. Almost all of these studies show that the programs provided substantial benefits in regard to children's self-esteem and social standing. Children who attended the classes also tended to perform well academically in subsequent grades, and several studies show that the participants were far less likely to be classified as learning disabled or in need of special services than children who were recommended for the programs but whose parents declined the recommendation. Parents of children who did participate expressed overwhelming approval of and support for the programs.

A few researchers have attempted to show that developmental extra-year programs do not provide *any* benefits. As is also explained in Dr. Uphoff's book, the best-known of these studies was a "meta-analysis" of other researchers' work, and in some cases this analysis interpreted their data in ways that contradicted the original researchers' own conclusions. This study also deliberately ignored all teacher and parent evaluations—including actual report card grades—because these measures of success might be "biased." Instead, this study relied on standardized achievement test scores from the primary grades, even though virtually every major organization of early childhood educators considers the standardized achievement test scores of young children to be unreliable. In addition, a number of positive studies were excluded from this meta-analysis, even though these positive studies were well known, well done, and readily accessible.

Unfortunately, in recent years seriously flawed research has also been used to advance political agendas in regard to numerous other education issues, such as vouchers, the teaching of reading, and even the overall performance of America's public schools. As a result, parents and teachers have to rely on common sense and a healthy skepticism when evaluating research claims, especially if the researchers have studied other studies, rather than actual children. Moreover, parents and teachers also have to remember that each child is a unique individual, not a statistical abstraction or average, and the key consideration when making placement decisions should always be the fit between an individual child and a specific class or grade.

Q. Should an additional year of learning time in a continuous-progress program be considered a form of retention?

A. No. Developmental extra-year classes are a positive alternative to retention—and a means of preventing retention from occurring in later grades.

Academic retention, also known as "flunking" or repeating a grade, usually occurs when a child has failed to meet the requirements for proceeding to the next grade. The child then spends another year in the same grade learning the same curriculum, having been "left back" with students who previously were a year behind. This can be a particularly difficult experience for older students, who have developed a stronger sense of group identity and social stigma.

In contrast, students participating in a continuous-progress program proceed with other children of the same age to a new class that has a new curriculum and a different teacher. This makes a developmental extra-year class a much more positive experience, as does the fact that this form of additional learning time usually enables students to experience success, instead of the frustration and failure that usually precede retention. In other words, a developmental extra-year class is a viable form of *early intervention* that prevents serious problems from arising, while retention is usually a *response* to serious problems that have already occurred.

These important differences should make it clear that attempts to classify continuous-progress extra-year classes as a form of retention are based more on political motivations than on the actual experiences of the students involved. While some critics have claimed that the classes are a form of retention, they have *never* produced even one research study showing that continuous-progress programs lead to the same sorts of outcomes as spending another year in the same grade. Anyone with a basic understanding of the English language and American schools should be able to grasp the distinction between these two forms of additional learning time, so any researcher or educator who confuses the two probably needs remediation or a career change.

In order to accommodate a wide range of students who have differing needs, schools should have continuous-progress extra-year classes and retention available as options. Having one without the other is almost sure to result in some students *not* having their needs met, and having neither option available can only result in the continued social promotion of students who have not learned needed material and therefore are not ready to succeed in the next grade.

Q.

Can continuous-progress extra-year programs help students achieve high standards?

A.

Yes. Continuous-progress extra-year classes are one of the keys to success in an era of high standards—for several reasons.

First and foremost, these classes provide many students with the additional time they need in order to learn the information and skills on which grade-level standards are based. This early intervention helps students develop a solid foundation of knowledge and skills—along with accompanying positive attitudes—all of which can enable the students to learn successfully and meet high standards throughout their years in school.

In addition, developmental extra-year classes can help students meet standards based on achievement test scores, simply because the additional learning and growing time enables students to take the tests when they are more mature. As noted earlier, many young children are not good at taking standardized tests, and their test scores may reflect their test-taking skills more than their understanding of grade-level material. Students who are more mature can often do better on these sorts of tests, especially when the tests are designed to measure reading comprehension and other higher-level thinking skills that some children need more time to develop.

Another benefit of continuous-progress extra-year programs in an era of high standards is that the programs provide a positive alternative for students who have *not* succeeded in meeting the standards at first. If students are required to meet high standards before proceeding to the next grade level, educators have a responsibility to provide effective programs for the students who *fail* to meet the standards. And knowing that retention in the upper grades often results in negative attitudes and experiences that can undermine any further school success, responsible educators need to offer alternative programs like continuous-progress extra-year classes—which let students move ahead with classmates to a new environment, where they will have the additional learning time and appropriate instruction they need before making a second attempt to meet the standards.

Educators cannot expect all their students to be promoted each year, unless the only standards for promotion are continued attendance and breathing. The reality in an era of high standards is that some students will need to participate in continuous-progress extra-year classes *before* they first try to meet the standards, and other students will need to participate in continuous-progress extra-year classes *after* they first try to meet the standards.

Looping & Multiage Classes in an Era of High Standards

Q. How do looping and multiage classes support the education and development of young children?

A. Looping and multiage classes are both effective ways of providing additional learning time for students, and building stronger relationships between teachers, students, and parents.

Looping occurs when a teacher stays with the same class for two or more years as the class moves on to new grade levels. For example, the teacher of a first grade class can return the following fall as the second grade teacher of the same class. The teacher and students can then pick up right where they left off in June, rather than having to spend a month or more getting to know one another and establishing new routines. In addition to making more effective use of the time available during the school year, looping also enables teachers and students to establish deeper and more stable working relationships, which can improve students' performance.

In a multiage classroom, the artificial barriers between grades are eliminated, and students can continue working in a continuous-progress educational environment with the same teacher for two or three years. As with looping, this approach provides additional learning time because the teacher does not have to spend the first month of the school year developing a working knowledge of and good relationship with the older students. Also, returning to the same classroom and teacher prevents students from having to go through a major transition and enables them to focus right away on learning new information and skills. The new students in the class can adjust more easily because they have older role models, who also benefit socially and emotionally from being the more senior and experienced members of a class.

Moreover, a multiage classroom can be a very supportive environment for children who need an additional year of learning time. These classes already contain children of different ages, who expect to remain with the same teacher for more than one year. And the distinct grade structure has been replaced by a continuous-progress educational environment, so some children can more easily *remain*—rather than *being retained*—for one additional year.

Looping and multiage classes are also more in sync with the way the students actually develop and learn. Rather than dividing young children's lives into distinct 36-week segments separated by "gateposts" and high-stakes decisions, looping and multiage classes allow the learning process to proceed in a more natural and effective way. This often leads to improved academic performance in the short term, and to the positive self-images and attitudes about learning that provide important long-term benefits.

Q.

A.

What types of learners are likely to benefit from looping and multiage classes?

All types of children can benefit from the additional learning time and stronger student-teacher relationships that looping and multiage classes provide. However, because of certain factors or circumstances, there are some children who are especially likely to benefit from looping or multiage classes.

As noted on the previous page, a multiage classroom can be an especially supportive environment for students who need an additional year of learning time. Whether the students are developmentally young, chronologically young, or have a deficit of knowledge or skills due to their backgrounds, the range of learners and emphasis on continuous progress in a multiage classroom can make it a particularly appropriate place for students who need an entire additional year to learn and grow. In addition, other students who need lesser amounts of additional time may find that the more efficient use of time in looping and multiage classes makes a crucial difference in their ability to learn and perform successfully.

Children who are especially likely to benefit from extended time with a caring and supportive adult should also be considered for a looping or multiage class. These types of students might include children from single-parent or dysfunctional families, children from families that have moved frequently, and children who have recently suffered the loss of a family member or friend. The deeper relationships and stable environments that looping and multiage classes can provide may prevent social and emotional disruptions from interfering with the learning of these sorts of children.

At the same time, it must also be noted that the benefits which looping and multiage classes can provide will be greatly diminished or lost altogether unless there is a healthy and appropriate mixture of students in the class. If a class is allowed to become dysfunctional because there are too many disruptive students, or if the class becomes a "dumping ground" for too many students whose special needs cannot be met by the additional learning time and extended relationships that these classes provide, the students will *not* be well served and the classes are likely to become discredited and avoided.

Knowing that all students can benefit from these classes and some students are especially likely to benefit from them, developmental educators have a responsibility to create the right mixture of students, as well as finding the best class for each individual student. If students are not ready for the curriculum and methods of instruction—or if students have a prolonged and intense conflict with the teacher that cannot be resolved—they should not be kept in these classes indefinitely. Flexible entrance and exit policies, along with follow-up studies, should be used to make sure that students truly do benefit from participation in these classes.

From *Developmental Education in an Era of High Standards* by Jim Grant. Published by Modern Learning Press, Inc., P.O. Box 167, Rosemont, NJ 08556, 1-800-627-5867. This page may be reproduced by the individual purchaser only for his or her own use.

Q. What are the characteristics of a high-quality looping or multiage classroom?

A. These types of classes share many of the same features with other high-quality classes at a school that uses a developmental approach to education. However, because high-quality looping and multiage classes are unique in certain respects, they do have some characteristics that are especially important.

As noted on the preceding pages, high-quality looping and multiage classes need to have an appropriate mixture of students, to prevent the classes from becoming dysfunctional or a "dumping ground." Flexible entrance and exit policies also need to be maintained in order for students to be able to join or leave the class as needed.

Another important characteristic is that the needs of students who have learning disabilities or who are gifted or talented are not neglected. Much as students who have disabilities must be evaluated and provided with an individualized education program that meets their needs, gifted or talented students also must have their needs met. And they should not spend too much of their time serving as "teacher's aides" and helping less advanced students.

In addition to the students, parent attitudes and behavior must also be seriously considered in a high-quality looping or multiage classroom. Parents who are strongly opposed to having their children placed in looping or multiage classes should not be forced to accept this sort of placement. Or if a prolonged personality clash that cannot be resolved develops between a teacher and parent, the teacher and parent should not be forced to continue interacting for more than one year.

Of course, teachers' attitudes and behavior are also an especially important consideration. Teachers who are opposed to this sort of assignment should never be forced to accept it, because their attitude will affect their work. And because the need to work effectively with such a wide range of students often makes teaching a looping or multiage class very challenging, marginal teachers should not be allowed to take on the challenge or continue teaching the same students for more than one year.

Overall, the developmental approach used in a high-quality looping or multiage class should be similar to that in other classes. Close attention should be paid to the developmental level of the students, their learning styles, and learning rates to make sure that the curriculum and methods of instruction are appropriate and effective.

And as with other types of classes, ongoing research and evaluation should be used to confirm the quality of looping or multiage classes. Students in the classes should be compared with similar students who did not participate in the classes, and these comparisons should continue through middle school and high school.

From *Developmental Education in an Era of High Standards* by Jim Grant. Published by Modern Learning Press, Inc., P.O. Box 167, Rosemont, NJ 08556, 1-800-627-5867. This page may be reproduced by the individual purchaser only for his or her own use.

Q. How should looping and multiage classes be integrated with other types of classes in a school?

A.
Like the developmental extra-year classes described in the previous chapter, looping and multiage classes are vital options which should be part of a range of educational environments provided by schools to meet the needs of today's diverse student population.

In order to be ready to educate a wide variety of learners effectively, schools need to be prepared to accommodate students who have reached different developmental levels, students who are learning at different rates, and students whose backgrounds have provided them with different amounts of information and skills (as well as different languages). With this sort of student population, there is *not* just one appropriate type of class; there are different types of classes that are right for different students.

Today's schools should therefore be ready to provide looping and multiage classes *in addition to* prekindergarten classes that provide an extra year of learning and growing time before kindergarten, and transition classes that provide an extra year between kindergarten and first grade as well as between later grades. However, there must also be standard grade-level classes for the students who are prepared to thrive in them, as well as for the parents who insist that their children should be in them. Otherwise, the lack of standard classes is likely to generate resistance and resentment among parents and educators who believe they are essential.

In addition, schools must also be prepared to have students remain an extra year in a standard grade-level class or a multiage class, when appropriate. As will be discussed further in the chapter on retention, there are some students in certain situations who benefit more from repeating a grade than from any other extra-time option.

Movement to and from different types of classes should be based on educators' recommendations and parents' decisions, with the understanding that situations can change quickly and drastically. Just as there need to be different types of classes for different students, students may need to switch from one type of class to another in different ways and for different reasons, rather than according to one master plan.

By providing different options for students (and choices for their parents), developmental educators greatly increase the odds that students will succeed in school and feel positive about learning and themselves, rather than struggling and failing because they did not fit into a single, highly standardized, and restrictive system.

Q. Can looping and multiage classes help students meet high standards?

A. Yes. Looping and multiage classes provide a variety of benefits that can lead to the improved learning and achievement required to meet high standards.

First and foremost, looping and multiage classes provide the additional learning time that many students need in order master basic skills and information. As noted earlier, the extended time spent together enables the teacher and students to get right back to work at the start of the second school year, rather than spending weeks getting to know one another, making transitions, and establishing new routines. And multiage classes provide a very comfortable environment for students who need an additional year of learning and growing time in order to meet high standards.

A teacher's in-depth knowledge and understanding of students during a second year can also lead to more effective instruction that increases the quantity and quality of a student's learning. This can be further enhanced by the stronger relationship that frequently develops between the teacher and students over an extended period. Children are often inspired to work harder by this sort of personal bond, which can also lead to fewer discipline problems and less absenteeism. These factors, of course, also result in more instructional and learning time.

Extended time with the same teacher will also result in parents becoming more involved in their children's education and having a more positive attitude about school. This not only can lead to the increased support that many children need from their parents, it can also lead students to develop a more positive attitude and a stronger desire to succeed academically, precisely because their parents are more enthusiastic about the teacher and the education their children are receiving.

More time to learn, more effective instruction, and better attitudes about school—clearly, these are key components of a successful effort to meet high standards.

Curriculum & Assessment in an Era of High Standards

Q.

What are the most important aspects of a developmental curriculum?

A.

A developmental curriculum is designed to teach students in ways that match the students' current developmental needs and capabilities, and support continued social, emotional, physical, and intellectual growth. In this way, it enables children to achieve initial success in school and then continue learning effectively.

It may seem obvious that the methods, materials, and concepts should be ones that the children can understand and work with effectively, but pressures to demonstrate early success, academic rigor, or the achievement of high standards can and do result in children struggling and failing in school because they are not yet ready for what and how they are being taught. A developmental curriculum, in contrast, helps children succeed in school and meet high standards precisely because the children are taught the right material in the right way and at the right time.

During early childhood, children start working with "hands-on," manipulative materials, which help them prepare to work with symbols such as words and numbers. Movement activities and imaginative play provide vital learning opportunities that support key areas of development. The use of learning centers allows children to work in a group or individually on a range of projects within a particular subject area. And a theme-based approach lets students focus on a topic of interest while integrating information and skills from a variety of subject areas.

As students progress through the elementary grades, the emphasis shifts to mastering information and skills through a balanced approach that combines a variety of instructional strategies. The methods and materials used are age-appropriate and compatible with recent research on the development of the brain. And at each grade level, educators remain responsive to different learning styles and learning rates, as well as to the varying levels of development and achievement in their classes.

Focusing on individual needs—and not just overall patterns of development—is particularly important with today's diverse student population. As David Elkind, Ph.D., states in his book *Reinventing Childhood*, "This does not mean that we must give up the effort to match curriculum and development, but that instead we need to couple this with a sensitive respect for individual differences. Put differently, *developmentally appropriate practice must be coupled with individually appropriate practice.*"

By matching students' developmental capabilities, individual needs, and personal interests, a developmental curriculum stimulates learning and involvement in education, while also helping students develop better attitudes about school and themselves. This all happens precisely because the curriculum is child-centered and not overly influenced by administrators, test designers, politicians, or other adults who are not directly involved in the education of the students.

Q.

Should a developmental curriculum rely on phonics instruction or a whole language approach?

A.

Both. A developmental curriculum uses a balanced approach to reading instruction, including phonics instruction and whole language strategies that help the full range of students in a class become competent and enthusiastic readers.

Comprehensive research studies have confirmed what many developmental educators have long known: students tend to benefit most when taught to read through a combination of methods. This enables children to "decode" some words by breaking them down into sounds and syllables; while also recognizing short, common "sight words" as whole words; and using the surrounding words to determine the meaning of still more words. Depriving students of any of these techniques puts them at a severe disadvantage in the upper grades, when they need to comprehend increasingly complex text in a limited amount of time.

A balanced approach to reading instruction is also important because it builds *both* competence and enthusiasm for reading. Phonics instruction was criticized and abandoned in earlier decades because it was often done in an excessively boring and regimented way, which left many students uninterested in reading. Then, some whole language purists became so concerned about making reading enjoyable and meaningful that they minimized or ignored the importance of teaching phonics and other skills. With a balanced approach, phonics and skills instruction can be linked to the literature children like, which helps them understand the value of what they are learning and motivates them to continue learning and reading.

As with so many other aspects of education, extremists who insist on an exclusive, "one-size-fits-all" approach to reading instruction ignore the differing needs of today's diverse student population. And an increasing number of educators and parents are recognizing that a balanced, common-sense approach to reading instruction is far more helpful to students than a continuation of the "reading wars," which like most wars have ended up turning at least some children into innocent victims.

A developmental approach to reading instruction also recognizes that just as children learn to read in different ways, some young children learn to read at different ages and rates. This should not automatically be interpreted as success or failure on the part of students or their teachers. Instead, it reflects the reality of a highly complex and challenging learning experience, combined with the varying development found among children in the same grade. Pushing young children to read too soon may actually interfere with their ability to read and lead to negative attitudes about reading, further undermining students' future learning and success.

Q.

How should writing be taught as part of a developmental curriculum?

A.

In the primary grades, writing instruction needs to be linked to the development of young children's physical abilities—especially using a pencil to form letters—as well as to the development of children's cognitive ability to communicate thoughts and ideas.

In preschool and kindergarten, children first should engage in activities such as coloring and drawing, which help them practice the muscle control and hand-eye coordination needed to write effectively with a pencil and paper. Children also need to learn basic concepts such as left-to-right progression and different sizes and shapes. As children develop the capability and interest required to begin communicating with words and pictures, they should be encouraged to do so and supported in their efforts. At this stage, approximations of letters and "inventive" spelling are acceptable and should not be allowed to inhibit children's enthusiasm for written communication.

As children progress through the grades, proper letter formation and correct spelling become more important, but the ultimate goal of written communication should also be emphasized and supported. Most developmental educators now use an approach known as the "writing process" to help children develop skills and the ability to communicate effectively and enjoyably. As part of this process, students write drafts of stories or essays, confer with the teacher and other students about their writing, practice editing and proofreading the drafts, and then "publish" a final version that is shared with classmates and others. By going through these stages of preparing a manuscript, students not only learn important skills, they also learn how to improve the overall quality and effectiveness of their writing.

Rather than rushing students into cursive (or script) handwriting, many experts recommend waiting until third grade to teach this new and more difficult form of writing. Not only does this give children more time for the muscular development needed to form slanted letters correctly, it also gives the children more time to master printing and to focus on the content of their written communication during second grade. Then, in third grade, most students are ready and eager to learn cursive.

In the past, some educators over-emphasized correct letter formation and spelling at too early an age. Then, other educators over-reacted by de-emphasizing or ignoring the importance of teaching correct letter formation and spelling in the later primary grades. As with other aspects of the curriculum, a successful approach to writing instruction neither starts too early nor is left until too late, because it is based on the students' developmental stages and individual learning rates.

Q. How should mathematics and science be taught as part of a developmental curriculum?

A. Children learn math and science naturally and well when they start by working with their senses and hands-on objects, and then make the transition to more abstract work with symbols and concepts in the later grades.

Young children are curious about the world around them and enjoy learning through exploration and play with blocks, water, sand, and a wide variety of other objects and materials that can be added, divided, measured, observed, transformed, and experimented with. This initial work enables children to start learning arithmetic and science effectively and successfully, providing a firm foundation on which more abstract learning can later be based.

Learning centers within a classroom can help students learn more about arithmetic and science through activities involving a variety of materials and activities. In addition to age-appropriate books and suggestions for projects, a science center might also include rocks, sea shells, magnets, fossils, plants, thermometers, and clocks, while a math center could include objects to count and weigh, cubes and other geometric shapes, graphing materials, and a flannel board.

As children grow older, they can begin to record and describe their observations and experiments, a well as make drawings of them. They can also read to obtain more information and solve problems expressed using words and concepts. This helps them expand their involvement with math and science, and understand the value and use of the full range of skills they are acquiring. Field trips that further extend the children's range of first-hand experiences are also extremely helpful.

As students begin to make the transition from physical manipulation of objects to mental manipulation of symbols, the curriculum should continue to support their natural interests and enthusiasms. This can be done through the use of themes and the presentation of information in diverse and relevant ways. At the same time, memorization and practice also need to be encouraged and integrated with other types of learning, in order to help children master new material and provide older students with the full range of knowledge and skills they need to succeed.

From *Developmental Education in an Era of High Standards* by Jim Grant. Published by Modern Learning Press, Inc., P.O. Box 167, Rosemont, NJ 08556, 1-800-627-5867. This page may be reproduced by the individual purchaser only for his or her own use.

Q. Are the arts an important part of a developmental curriculum?

A. Yes. The arts are a very important, integral part of a developmental curriculum, and they should not be treated as lesser subjects or extra-curricular activities. Throughout the primary grades and beyond, the arts are extremely useful aids in developing children's skills and expanding their understanding, as well as stimulating creative expression.

Visual arts are especially important when children are learning to write and read. Children need to draw and color as part of the process of learning to write, and in the later primary grades illustrating written work helps students continue to develop their communication skills. Picture books help children learn to read, and then paintings and photographs continue to provide valuable information and perspectives on different cultures and historical eras. Of course, these visual images also have an essential role in introducing children to fine art and helping them develop their sense of aesthetics.

Music is another important and helpful element of a developmental curriculum. Singing helps children learn about language, time, and rhythm, and it facilitates group participation. The playing of musical instruments can provide many of the same benefits, and listening to recorded music can help set the mood for quiet times or energetic activities, as well as add an important dimension to themes.

Acting and dance can also help young children develop physical and mental capabilities. Vital concepts such as left and right or backward and forward can be internalized by moving through space in an organized way. Then, these sorts of activities can help children develop a better understanding of books, other cultures, and their own capabilities.

The widespread recognition of the importance of different learning styles provides added support for making the arts an integral part of a developmental curriculum. Educators need to provide information and activities that utilize all three "modalities"—visual, auditory, and kinesthetic—in order to meet the needs of the full range of students in their classes. Clearly, the arts are an effective and important way to do this. Moreover, many developmental educators now recognize the importance of helping students develop what Howard Gardner has called *multiple intelligences*. Three of these intelligences are musical, spatial, and bodily/kinesthetic, which can obviously be fostered through involvement with the arts.

Even when an educator is more concerned about academic performance than artistic development, personal fulfillment, or a combination of all three, the arts can make a vital contribution and should be a valued part of the curriculum.

Q. Should computers be part of a developmental curriculum?

A. Yes. Computers can play a valuable role in a developmental curriculum. But for young children in particular, computers should not be used as a substitute for interaction with a caring adult. In addition, computers should not be used as a substitute for work with the senses and hands-on objects, or for the time needed to develop and mature.

Computers can stimulate young children's interest in learning and help the children gain access to information. High-quality educational software can enable students to engage in self-directed activities and obtain programmed feedback. And, of course, having children work with computers can help them become competent and feel comfortable with tools that are likely to be essential for higher learning and successful careers.

On the other hand, computers require the use of a keyboard or mouse—and rely on symbols, images, and "virtual reality"—rather than providing the firsthand experience with real objects that is an essential part of a developmental curriculum for young children. Moreover, today's educational computers are primarily a visual medium, with sound playing more of a secondary role, so children whose primary style is auditory or tactile/kinesthetic are not as likely to benefit from their use. Perhaps most importantly, so many of today's children already spend too much time sitting in front of television screens and video games, and the use of a computer results in even more time spent sitting in front of a machine, rather than interacting directly with peers or caring adults.

As students progress through the grades, computers can become exciting research tools that stimulate further reading and writing, and support other educational activities, as well. Even then, however, supervision and care are needed. Many parents find they have to establish limits on older students' use of computers at home, because valuable homework time may be spent playing games, electronically "chatting," or engaging in other activities that have little or no educational value. Schools and libraries have also found that computers and their internet connections may be used by students for purposes that are wasteful, dangerous, or even illegal.

While computers should be part of children's education, in some cases concerns about academic competition and future careers—supported by the marketing campaigns of profit-driven computer companies—have led to excessive or inappropriate use of computers by students. As with other aspects of a developmental curriculum, the successful use of educational computers requires continued understanding of and focusing on the actual needs and capabilities of our children.

Q. How should students' learning and achievement be evaluated?

A. Evaluations used as part of a developmental approach should provide accurate information about children's process and progress over time. This information can help teachers and parents support the development and education of children, and give the children important feedback about their work.

Children in the primary grades are developing at a rapid pace and learning at different rates, so capabilities they did *not* have at one point may appear soon thereafter. That's why it is important to compare a child's current accomplishments with previous efforts, not just the accomplishments of other children in the same grade. A child who was lagging behind classmates may experience a growth spurt and then surge ahead, while another child who seemed quite advanced may enter a stage in which academic progress slows for reasons unrelated to intelligence and effort.

Evaluations used as part of a developmental approach should also match the curriculum in their content and format. Evaluations of this sort are known as *authentic assessments*, because they show what children actually do in school, rather than how the children respond to contrived questions presented in an unfamiliar and unnatural format. Probably the best-known and most widely accepted form of authentic assessment is a *portfolio* of student work—which can include samples of writing and artwork, tape recordings of the student reading aloud, lists of books the student has read, excerpts from or photographs of projects, and other documentary information. Other types of authentic assessment include checklists and anecdotal records maintained by teachers, and demonstrations or displays by students.

Authentic assessments have added value because they are an effective means of sharing information with parents, who can then have a better understanding of what their children are doing and where help is needed. Another important benefit is that authentic assessments do not require changes in the curriculum, because they are an integral part of it. When the evaluation of young children is based on formal tests instead, valuable instructional time is usually devoted to familiarizing children with the test format. This process is known as "teaching to the test" and can help some students achieve better scores, but because many young children simply have trouble performing stressful pencil-and-paper tasks under tight time constraints, the scores may simply measure how well the students take tests, rather than what the students actually know and achieve.

As children grow more skilled, experienced, and knowledgeable, formal testing can provide more accurate information about students' achievement and comparative standing. Even then, however, the pressure to teach to the test can have a negative impact on the curriculum and on the students' actual learning.

Q. How should report cards be integrated with a developmental approach to education?

A. Report cards should provide accurate information about young children's progress over time, and the information on the report card should be presented in a way that will help parents and their children make use of it.

Just as evaluations should be derived from the curriculum, report cards should be based on goals or standards set for the students by their teachers and administrators. These goals or standards can include broad objectives related to communication, understanding, attitude, and the acquisition of skills, as well as more detailed objectives related to specific subject areas.

In addition to determining the goals or standards, developmental educators also have to determine how best to provide information about the students' achievements and progress. Traditional letter grades (A, B, C, D, F) have limited value in this respect, because quantifying young children's diverse educational activities and then summarizing them as a single letter is difficult and does not provide much useful information. This sort of grading system may also make children reluctant to engage in needed trial-and-error learning or take creative risks, for fear their grades may be lower as a result. In addition, a single letter grade can become a self-fulfilling prophecy that leads young children not to like a subject and then continue to do poorly at it, simply because their initial letter grades convinced them that they were "not good" at it.

Instead of letter grades, descriptive phrases can provide information that more accurately reflects the complexity of young children's development and learning process. Phrases that focus on frequency ("Some of the time" or "Most of the time") or progression over time ("Not yet" or "Beginning") provide both information and perspective, and can still be used in a checklist format. Other phrases, such as "Needs improvement," can identify areas of concern without labeling a student's achievements or behavior. Additional factors, such as whether a child does well without much effort or works hard but encounters little success, should also be part of the information reported.

As children progress through the grades, the types of report cards they receive can and should change in response to the goals and standards for the grades, what and how the students are learning, and what information would be most helpful to their parents. Like the curriculum and the evaluations used to measure student performance, report cards should be child-centered and reflect the developmental progression that naturally occurs over time.

Q. How should standardized achievement tests be integrated with a developmental approach to education?

A. Very carefully—and only when students are old enough for the test scores to be accurate and have value, which is usually around fourth grade. Even then, standardized tests scores may be misleading, and an over-emphasis on them can have a negative effect on student learning and achievement.

As noted earlier in this chapter, young children are *not* good at taking formal tests, because they are still learning to read, write, and concentrate under pressure, as well as sit still for extended periods of time. In addition, some young children who are developing more slowly—or who have not had much previous exposure to the words and concepts on which standardized tests are based—may do poorly on these tests despite above-average intelligence and effort.

These problems are compounded by the fact that standardized tests are very limited in what they measure and how they measure it. Skills and subject areas measured by a standardized test must be capable of being carefully defined and quantified. Other capabilities and factors that also determine success in school—such as a student's creativity, interest in a subject, desire to succeed, and long-term patterns of success or failure—cannot be measured in this way.

As a result, standardized test scores should be viewed as "snapshots" that provide temporary and limited information about older students. These tests should *not* be administered to students before third grade and should *never* be used as the sole basis for deciding whether to promote a student to the next grade level. Standardized test scores should also *not* be used as the sole basis for revamping a curriculum, having a state "seize control" of a school, or any other high-stakes action. Standardized tests are not designed or suited for these purposes.

As was also noted earlier, familiarizing students with the format and typical content of these tests can improve scores, so the amount of emphasis placed on these scores often influences the amount of time teachers devote to related practice and drills. Time that could have been spent on meaningful and effective instruction may therefore be devoted to test-preparation activities that have little educational value—and result in cynical and outright negative attitudes on the part of students, who see that artificial exercises and "beating the system" are a high priority.

Once students have reached the age when standardized tests can provide valid comparative measures, test scores can help confirm the value of a developmental approach. But even then, the results must be looked at over several years, so the strengths or weaknesses of students in one specific grade are not misinterpreted.

From *Developmental Education in an Era of High Standards* by Jim Grant. Published by Modern Learning Press, Inc., P.O. Box 167, Rosemont, NJ 08556, 1-800-627-5867. This page may be reproduced by the individual purchaser only for his or her own use.

Q. How can a developmental approach to curriculum and assessment help students meet high standards?

A. A developmental curriculum and authentic assessments are vital means of helping students to learn effectively—and to feel good about school and themselves—so they have the knowledge, skills, and positive attitudes needed to meet high standards.

By providing students with the right curriculum at the right time, a developmental approach enables children to learn well, make continuous progress, and experience school success. Authentic assessments support this process by providing valuable information about students' actual performance in school, so educators, parents, and the students themselves can identify strengths and weaknesses, and then determine how to make needed improvements.

Of course, a developmental approach helps students meet high standards only if the standards are realistic and derived from the students' true needs and capabilities, just as the curriculum and assessments are. When unrealistic standards are imposed for political or other reasons, *no* approach will work successfully. A developmental curriculum may help some kindergartners learn to count to one hundred, for example, but if overly ambitious politicians and bureaucrats want kindergarten students to develop an understanding of numbers up to five hundred, as was proposed in Virginia, the developmental curriculum and students may be considered "failures," when actually it was the creators of the standards who failed to do their job.

This is similar to what happened in the late 1950s, when concerns about the Soviet Union's lead in the "space race" led to the creation of the "push-down" curriculum, which resulted in more intensive academic instruction in the primary grades and a corresponding increase in student failure and other problems. The threat of foreign competition was used as an excuse to make the primary grade curriculum more academic and less developmental again in the 1980s, when Japan seemed to be becoming dominant economically, and in the early 1990s, when America was supposed to prepare for the "new world order" and the "information age." Now, of course, the Soviet Union no longer exists, Japan has had prolonged economic problems, and rather than facing a new world order, America continues to dominate a range of information-based industries, including computers, finance, and biotechnology.

This does not mean we should rest on our laurels, but it does indicate that our standards should reflect the actual capabilities of young Americans, rather than being used to alter our children in a vain attempt to respond to some threat that will probably be obsolete by the time the children reach high school.

From *Developmental Education in an Era of High Standards* by Jim Grant. Published by Modern Learning Press, Inc., P.O. Box 167, Rosemont, NJ 08556, 1-800-627-5867. This page may be reproduced by the individual purchaser only for his or her own use.

Special Needs in an Era of High Standards

Q. What are special needs?

A. Special needs are disabilities that require students to receive additional assistance in order to obtain a full education. These disabilities may be obvious physical disabilities, such as deafness or blindness, which prevent children from participating in the full range of regular classroom activities. Or the disabilities may be extremely difficult to detect and may not have any clear physical causes, but still require early and effective intervention.

Physical disabilities need not be as extreme as blindness or deafness to warrant intervention. Children who have limited but untreated visual or auditory problems— or intermittent problems—are at a severe disadvantage when learning to read, write, and follow instructions. But because many young children are still developing the ability to focus their eyes and to understand and respond to spoken words, accurate diagnosis can be difficult.

Learning disabilities, such as dyslexia, also make effective learning and academic performance far more difficult, and may also prove difficult to detect. Dyslexic students may have trouble distinguishing *b* from *d*, 6 from 9, and left from right. They may also write and speak words in a confusing order. But again, these sorts of mistakes are also made by many young children who are not dyslexic. The difference is that dyslexic students are unlikely to outgrow such errors if their disability is left undiagnosed and untreated. A learning disability that has recently caused widespread concern and controversy is an Attention Deficit Disorder (ADD), which causes increased difficulty in focusing attention and staying on task. Of course, this is also a characteristic of some young children who do not have ADD.

Emotional and social problems may also be officially classified as "conduct disorders" or other special needs that require treatment at school, because they prevent a child from learning and interacting well. These sorts of disabilities may result from physical causes, dysfunctional family environments, exposure to dangerous substances, or other problems that affect a child's development and behavior.

In recent years, identifying and treating children's special needs have become more challenging, because many of today's children have multiple, co-occurring special needs, rather than just one disability. For example, instead of simply having dyslexia, young child may be found to have dyslexia, ADD, and a conduct disorder, as well as bouts of depression that may or may not be related to the child's other disabilities.

While special needs are usually found only among a small minority of a school's population, the educational problems they can cause—and the difficulty and expense of treating them—can have a major impact on other students, as well.

Q. How should developmental educators participate in the detection of special needs?

A. Detecting and responding to special needs is a very important aspect of early childhood education, because some disabilities may not become apparent until children reach school age and begin to participate in formal classroom activities. Early childhood educators therefore have a special responsibility to remain alert for disabilities and to help identify special needs, while also providing a supportive environment for children who have a wide range of needs and capabilities.

Screening for certain types of special needs is mandated by federal law. Well-trained specialists using validated screening instruments should evaluate every student beginning elementary school. Those students who may have special needs should receive further evaluation through specialized diagnostic examinations. Meanwhile, other special needs may neither be covered by federal law nor detected by initial screenings, so developmental educators must have a thorough understanding of the warning signs for special needs and continue paying close attention to their students.

Developmental educators are likely to be adept at distinguishing children who may need assistance from those who are just exhibiting certain characteristics associated with a particular developmental stage. This is especially important because educators also have a responsibility not to mislabel students. And studies have shown that children who are chronologically younger than their peers are more likely to be diagnosed as "learning disabled." Children who are developing at a slower but still normal rate may also be diagnosed as learning disabled if not properly screened.

The link between time to develop and the diagnosis of special needs was confirmed by studies cited in *Real Facts from Real Schools*, by James Uphoff, Ed.D., which showed that children who received an additional year of learning time in an extra-year program were less likely to be diagnosed as learning disabled than students who were recommended for the program but went on to the next grade level instead. In a similar way, if efforts to impose high standards result in an accelerated curriculum for primary grade students, there is a risk that more children will be classified as learning disabled because they are so unprepared for—or biologically incapable of—more advanced work at an early age.

Effective communication is also an important responsibility for developmental educators when a child is suspected of having a disability. They need to coordinate with specialists and administrators at the school, and with the parents, who are very likely to need and want information and support. Developmental educators also need to obtain background information from the parents that can contribute to an accurate diagnosis and, if necessary, appropriate treatment.

Q. What steps should be taken after a child is found to have special needs?

A. Special needs may require a variety of services that will be provided by different personnel. A developmental educator must therefore be prepared to serve as a coordinator and communicator, as well as a teacher.

Federal legislation mandates the preparation of an Individual Eduction Plan (IEP) for all disabled children. The IEP must first provide for the child to have access to appropriate educational facilities, and it then outlines academic and behavioral goals, as well as the strategies and methods designed to attain them. It is usually prepared by a "child study team" that includes the child's teacher, the school psychologist, and other specialists. The parents may also be involved in the preparation of an IEP, and if not, they should certainly review it with the child's teacher. It should then continue to be reviewed periodically and always remain open to revision.

One of the most important and controversial questions for educators and parents is the type of program that will best meet the needs of the child. In the past, children who were disabled usually attended special schools that had smaller classes run by specially trained teachers. This approach is still used and appropriate for children who have severe disabilities that prevent them from functioning effectively in a regular classroom.

Some children with less severe disabilities may benefit from placement in a regular classroom, which they may leave at times for "pull-out" sessions with a specialist. Or they may remain in the classroom and have a specialist join them for individual or small-group sessions. Finally, some children with disabilities participate in "full inclusion" programs that leave them in a regular classroom without additional assistance.

Unfortunately, some people have come to view a disabled child's placement as an ideological or civil rights issue, rather than an educational issue. And, as always, there are extremists who do not want to let the realities and limitations of individual children, teachers, and schools interfere with their personal beliefs.

To best meet the special needs of a specific child, a realistic, common-sense approach is needed, based on the fit between the child and the school he or she will be attending. In addition, educators have a responsibility to meet the instructional needs of *all* the children in the class, not just the students who have special needs. If classmates' needs are not being met because one or two children are receiving an unfair amount of attention and support from the teacher, many students' learning and performance will decrease, and a negative and competitive environment that adversely affects all the students is also likely to result.

Q. What factors should be considered when making decisions about the placement of a child who has special needs?

A. In his book *Reinventing Childhood*, psychologist David Elkind identifies several variables that can affect the placement of a child who has special needs. As Dr. Elkind states in the book, "Years of experience with inclusion have tended to show that the real issue is not whether inclusion is right or wrong, but rather *under what circumstances inclusion is likely to be successful*."

1. **The child's special needs and developmental levels**—The extent of a child's disabilities should always be the primary concern. A child who has a single, relatively mild disability may function well and feel comfortable in a regular classroom, but a child who has a severe disability or multiple co-occurring problems may suffer academically and emotionally from being in the same type of classroom. And rather than focusing just on disabilities, educators and parents also need to consider the child's overall intellectual, physical, and social/emotional development.

2. **The preparation of the child and the teacher for inclusion**—A child who has had previous, successful experiences in regular classes or similar groups is likely to do well, but a child who has been receiving only individual attention or participating only in smaller special-needs classes may find the transition to a regular class overwhelming. In a similar way, a teacher who is well prepared to include disabled children in a regular classroom will be able to provide more effective help than a teacher who has not received proper training.

3. **The teacher-to-children ratio and percentage of children who have special needs**—A teacher who has only 16 children in a class can obviously provide more individual attention to a disabled child than a teacher who has 27 children. Classes for special-needs children are kept small precisely because the students *each* need so much individual attention, and as the number of special-needs children included in a regular classroom increases, the amount of individual attention each child will receive is likely to decrease further.

4. **The availability of specialists**—Specialists not only can supplement the classroom teacher's instruction, they also can free the teacher to work with other students. However, in some schools specialists are only available on a very limited basis, which is likely to result in less individualized attention and effective instruction for all the children in a regular classroom.

By thoughtfully and realistically considering these variables, educators and parents can make the best possible decisions for all the children in their care.

Q. Does a developmental approach to education help children who have special needs?

A. Yes. Children who have special needs are more likely to thrive when they are working with a developmental curriculum and teachers who are focused on meeting students' developmental and individual needs.

Work and play with hands-on materials are essential building blocks in the intellectual development of all children. But when children have learning disabilities that interfere with their processing of abstract symbols and information, initial work with hands-on materials is even more important. Additional work of this sort may then be needed to help learning-disabled students make the transition to the mental manipulation of letters and numbers.

As Priscilla Vail points out in her book *Learning Styles*, many children who have trouble with two-dimensional symbols like letters and numbers do very well at three-dimensional activities, which can range from sports and drama to engineering and medicine. So, developmental learning experiences that involve drawing, coloring, music, movement, and drama not only can help learning disabled children develop valuable skills, these experiences can also help the children enjoy the sort of success that is far more difficult for them to achieve through pencil-and-paper tasks.

Most of all, developmental educators are prepared to work with a variety of different developmental stages and capabilities, and their classes are designed to help a wide range of students make progress and achieve success. A developmental approach also recognizes that children learn at different rates, so it includes time-flexibility options and an evaluation system that focuses on progress over time, all of which can help meet the individual needs of learning-disabled students. This is far different from a more traditional and unforgiving approach geared to either the best students or average students, which can emphasize or even exacerbate the difficulties of children who have special needs.

Another benefit of the developmental approach is that it emphasizes children's social, emotional, and physical development, rather than focusing just on intellectual development. These other aspects of development can have an especially powerful effect—either positive or negative—on children whose intellectual development may be slower or more challenging than that of other children who have reached the same age.

Q. Do children with special needs benefit from having an additional year to learn and grow in school?

A. Usually. An additional year to learn and grow can help learning-disabled children who need more time to succeed in school, but not every learning-disabled child needs an additional year. And additional learning and growing time should *never* be used as a substitute for other special education services that meet the specific needs of learning-disabled children.

Children who have special needs may also be developmentally young, or they may be some of the chronologically youngest children in a grade. As discussed earlier in the book, a child who is developmentally or chronologically young is more likely to struggle and fail in school, and when either or both of these factors are combined with a learning disability, a child is very likely to be at risk for school failure. An additional year to learn and grow—combined with other interventions designed to meet the child's other needs—can prove very helpful for this sort of child.

Other learning-disabled children may come from backgrounds that deprived them of adequate exposure to basic information or readiness skills. There are also children whose special needs have prevented them from learning grade-level information and skills in school, and who therefore are not ready to succeed in subsequent grades. For children such as these, an additional year to learn and grow—combined with other interventions designed to meet the children's other needs—can help them master the knowledge and skills needed to learn well and succeed as they proceed through the upper grades.

However, in today's budget-conscious environment, some schools and districts prohibit what they call "double-dipping." They will allow a child to receive special services *or* an additional year of learning time, but not both. Unfortunately, this sort of policy is based on budgetary considerations rather than the actual educational needs of the student. And this sort of policy is short-sighted even from a financial perspective, because providing one needed intervention without the other is likely to result in long-term problems that require even more spending and lead to less success.

A further risk is that the lack of success which results from providing special-needs students with *only* an additional year of learning time may then be used to discredit the value of providing an additional year of school for *any* students—learning disabled or not. The same thing can happen if an additional year is given to learning-disabled students who do not need it, or if extra-year classes are allowed to become "dumping grounds" filled with special-needs students who should be receiving other services.

Q. What should be done about "gray-area" children who appear to have special needs but do not qualify for existing programs?

A. Teachers across America are reporting that an alarming number of children appear to be learning disabled but do *not* meet the established criteria for receiving special needs support. Clearly, these children need and deserve to have their special needs met, for their own sake and for the sake of all their classmates.

One major cause of this problem is the tightening of disability criteria for financial reasons, rather than educational reasons. In an effort to reduce spending on special education, some states and districts have imposed statistical limits on the number of students who can be classified as learning disabled. There are also schools where an unofficial cap on the number of special-needs students may result in decisions not to refer or classify students who in other locations would routinely be designated as learning impaired. As a result, new arrivals, students whose special needs are discovered at a later date, or students whose needs are not easily classified may not receive appropriate assistance simply because of a special needs "quota." Unfortunately, there are also situations where some sort of learning disability appears to exist but cannot be identified or defined according to official criteria, despite the best efforts and intentions of the educators and specialists involved.

These trends have been compounded by the growing number of children whose learning and performance capabilities have been affected by multiple, co-occurring factors and circumstances. Individually, these factors and circumstances might not qualify as special needs, but their combined effects can disable a student to an even greater extent than a single, clearly defined, and routinely accepted disability that has a limited impact. In many cases, the home environment of this sort of student is clearly a factor, and the underlying causes of the learning problems might include a dysfunctional family situation that leads to a loss of income, poor nutrition, lack of medical care, violence, neglect, frequent changes of address, and excessive television watching. While these problems themselves are not considered disabilities, the characteristics associated with them, such as difficulty focusing and paying attention, frequent acting out in the classroom, and trouble communicating with others, are the same as those associated with officially recognized disabilities.

To help gray-area children learn and perform well in school, decisions about special services should be based on the individual educational needs of the child, not on finances or statistics. There must also be official recognition that gray-area children exist and their numbers are growing, so that valid policies and procedures can be developed for them. In addition, coordination between educators and other providers of social services is needed to address any family-related causes of special needs.

From *Developmental Education in an Era of High Standards* by Jim Grant. Published by Modern Learning Press, Inc., P.O. Box 167, Rosemont, NJ 08556, 1-800-627-5867. This page may be reproduced by the individual purchaser only for his or her own use.

Q. How should the emphasis on achieving high standards affect the education of children who have special needs?

A.
As with children who do *not* have special needs, high standards should serve as a means of improving the learning and performance of disabled children. The introduction of reasonable standards that take into account both individual and developmental differences can have this desirable effect.

Setting standards that learning-disabled students *can* meet encourages them to work hard, and it introduces an element of accountability for them and their educators by making sure the students learn needed, appropriate material. Reasonable standards also provide a framework for making decisions about promoting students to a new grade or providing additional learning time. This, in turn, facilitates instruction and learning, because when all the children in a class have a similar foundation of knowledge and skills, the teacher can spend much less time on material that some students already know or that others may not yet be ready to learn successfully.

The problem, of course, is that creating standards which take into account individual differences and needs is very difficult and time-consuming. It is far easier to create a single set of standards and require that *all* the students in a district or state meet the same standards. Unfortunately, this sort of standard setting, with the accompanying mandates and resulting legal challenges, has already occurred and is likely to continue, even though it is neither reasonable nor fair.

It would obviously be unfair to require a physically disabled student in a wheelchair to compete in a race that requires jumping over hurdles and going uphill in the same amount of time as a student who has full use of his or her legs. Yet for a student with severe dyslexia or a similar learning disability, learning to read can be an uphill battle that requires the surmounting of numerous hurdles and is very likely to take additional time. To insist that this student meet the same high standards as other students who have no such disability can result in severe frustration and repeated failure for the student, and it may also have negative consequences for educators and schools that are evaluated on this same unfair basis. Moreover, if learning-disabled students are automatically denied promotion to a new grade solely on the basis of standardized test scores, there will also be negative consequences for the politicians and taxpayers who must provide the funds required for the students to repeat a grade, which in many cases will be a totally unnecessary and inappropriate waste of money.

The reality is that standards can only help to improve learning and achievement when they take into account individual differences and special needs.

Students, Teachers, & Parents in an Era of High Standards

Q. How many students should be in a primary grade classroom?

A. Ideally, a kindergarten class should have less than 20 students. A first grade, second grade, or multiage class should have no more than 25 students. And if a significant proportion of the students in the class have special needs, the class size should be even smaller.

Classes of this size allow teachers to have an appropriate amount of one-to-one instructional contact with each student, and to individualize the curriculum and teaching methods accordingly. These class sizes also enable a teacher to maintain discipline more effectively, in part because they minimize competition for attention from the teacher, which can sometimes result in students misbehaving simply to capture the teacher's attention.

Overly large class sizes require a teacher to rely more on whole-class and small-group instruction, which are always appropriate in some situations but are often used more in large classes simply because of the increased demands on the teacher's time and attention. And the corresponding lack of individualized instruction can easily result in students *not* receiving the specific help they need, or even *not* having their specific needs identified.

Several large, controlled research studies have shown that smaller class sizes provide significant benefits. In particular, as reported in the May, 1992 issue of *The American School Board Journal*, *"Well-controlled, longitudinal research on Project STAR and the Lasting Benefits Study indicates that smaller class sizes can provide substantial gains in student achievement, especially in the early grades. The results can include higher self-esteem among students and higher morale among teachers—plus lower retention rates and less need for special education facilities."*

Of course, it should come as no surprise that a few researchers have managed to compile data that would *seem* to show a teacher can educate 35 or 40 students just as well as 20 students—in the exact same amount of time. These days, there is almost always some contradictory research, especially when there may be significant financial and career advantages for researchers who analyze (or manipulate) data in a particular way. Smaller class sizes do require a bigger budget than large classes, and there are organizations that promote research which will help them oppose increased funding for public schools.

Just as when "expert witnesses" offer totally contradictory testimony at a trial, people need to use their own common sense and firsthand experience to decide which evidence seems the most realistic and convincing. And if any grown-ups really think they can work just as effectively with 35 children as with 20 children, I would suggest they try doing it once or twice to see for themselves.

Q. Should recess be a regular part of the school day for elementary school students?

A. Yes. Regularly scheduled recess supports the education and development of students in a number of ways. Eliminating recess, in contrast, can have a very negative impact on students' academic performance and behavior.

Young children's physical development does not just support the development of athletic skills, it also supports the development of academic skills, such as the hand-eye coordination needed for writing. In many elementary schools, physical education classes are limited to one day per week, so recess provides a vital opportunity for young children to exercise and develop their physical abilities. This activity also enables many students to use up energy that might otherwise lead to behavior problems and interfere with concentration and "seat work."

In addition to the obvious physical, emotional, and academic advantages, recess also provides other important benefits. Unstructured time in which children can develop their imaginations and interact with each other has become increasingly rare, as parents' busy schedules result in many children spending extended amounts of time in closely supervised child-care activities, or simply watching television and playing video games. Recess provides an appropriate time for children to develop their imaginations and social skills, which can be vital to later career success.

When schools eliminate recess, some children may benefit from the additional instructional time but lose out on the other benefits that recess can provide. Many other children may *not* even benefit from the additional instructional time, because their physical and emotional frustration prevents them from concentrating and performing well academically.

The emphasis on achieving high standards has led a few educators to believe they are helping their students by making school a place of "all work and no play." Sadly, this short-sighted approach is likely to result in *fewer* students achieving high standards, because it creates so many other problems for the children. There have also been some claims that recess had to be eliminated for safety reasons, but the fact that schools in all sorts of neighborhoods throughout America have found ways to provide recess safely indicates that this is likely to be an unconvincing excuse.

I have long been an outspoken advocate of providing additional learning time for children who need it, but eliminating recess is the wrong way to provide extra time. Knowing that some educators punish children by making them stay inside during recess, the permanent elimination of recess should be recognized as a cruel and unusual punishment that also happens to be counter-productive, rather than an educational enhancement.

Q.

Can inappropriate standards and their impact on a curriculum result in increased student misbehavior and discipline problems?

A.

Yes. Even when recess and physical education classes are provided in elementary school, the pressures and frustration created by the miseducation of young children can often lead them to "act out" in disruptive ways.

Virtually all young children want to learn and can learn. As long as the curriculum and methods of instruction are in sync with students' developmental and individual needs, the students' natural curiosity and enthusiasm will usually lead them to learn well and enjoy the process. However, when children cannot succeed in a classroom because the type of instruction and materials being used actually *prevent* them from learning, the thwarted desire to learn and accompanying negative attitudes may result in frustration and anger being directed at the teacher and at other students.

This is especially likely to occur when active young children are forced to spend too much time sitting still and doing fine-motor tasks. Students' traditional inclination to move and talk as they learn has in many cases been exacerbated by overly permissive parents, who have not had the willingness or understanding needed to teach children proper behavior and social skills. In addition, teachers have also reported an increase in the number of children who have difficulty paying attention and staying on task, which may result in part from excessive television watching that has habituated children to instant gratification and rapid-fire changes of topic. These trends make an overly formal curriculum all the more inappropriate for many young children, who are likely to become "discipline problems" simply because they are having so much difficulty adapting to school.

Rather than forcing children to "bottle up" their energy until recess, gym, or the end of the school day, teachers can intersperse regular intervals of vigorous movement with their more formal academic instruction. This can allow children to use up some of their energy, release their stress, and relax their minds and their eyes, so they will then be better prepared to sit, concentrate, and focus once again. And if the movement is linked to the curriculum in a creative way, it can reinforce the instruction.

Most of all, if an increase in misbehavior and discipline problems occurs, educators should re-evaluate their curriculum and methods of instruction and consider modifying them to meet students' needs more effectively. However, in today's real-world classrooms, teachers may have no choice but to implement an overly academic curriculum and attempt to train children to meet high standards. The teachers then need to demonstrate more than ever that they understand and care for their students, by continuing to act fairly and be supportive while also setting firm limits.

Q. What role should parents play in a school that uses a developmental approach?

A. Parents are welcome and vital members of a school community, and they can make very valuable contributions to the developmental approach to education.

Many parents intuitively recognize the validity of key aspects of a developmental approach, such as the importance of intellectual, physical, and social/emotional development; the need to match the curriculum and instruction to children's developmental capabilities; and the value of providing additional learning time for children who need it. The support provided by understanding parents can be a tremendous help in sustaining and improving this sort of approach. However, other parents may need to learn the value of this approach, and in this era of high standards, some parents may actively push for a more accelerated academic curriculum.

Ongoing communication with all parents is therefore a vital part of a developmental approach to education. A very effective way to build positive relationships is to have a meeting with parents in the classroom at the start of the school year. Being in the classroom makes it easier for a teacher to explain and demonstrate the various components of a developmental approach. Establishing a parent lending library and providing handouts that explain the benefits of a developmental approach—as well as the negative affects of an overly accelerated academic curriculum—can also help enormously, as can parent newsletters.

Sign-up sheets that solicit parent involvement in class activities should be prominently displayed at the first parent meeting. Parents are more likely to be supportive when they see firsthand how much and how well students are learning, as well as how hard the teacher works. Parent involvement can range from acting as an aide on a regular basis to helping occasionally with specialized tasks such as publishing a student book, staging a play, or being a chaperon during a field trip. And when parents then receive verbal and/or written thanks from the students and teacher for helping in these ways, they are all the more likely to value the way their children are being taught.

This type of involvement also helps parents provide appropriate support for homework assignments and other projects, and to respond effectively to report cards and information provided during conferences. It also helps the teacher get to know the parents as unique individuals and develop a better understanding of them and their child.

Q. How can teachers foster administrators' support for developmental education in an era of high standards?

A. Today's school administrators are under intense pressure to show that their students are meeting high standards. So, teachers need to show their administrators how a developmental approach helps students achieve more in school.

First and foremost, administrators need to understand and see for themselves how a developmental curriculum produces better readers and writers than a more formal academic curriculum that is combined with extensive test preparation activities. Teachers need to demonstrate that their approach develops third and fourth graders who can truly comprehend what they are reading and can therefore score well on high-stakes tests at that time, while a curriculum based on intensive skill drills from an early age may result in older students who can sound out words but don't know what they mean, and who therefore start to flounder and fail in the crucial later grades.

In addition, administrators need to understand how time-flexibility options such as transition classes and retention can help some students and their schools meet high standards. Developmental educators have to explain how providing additional learning and growing time can be the most effective and appropriate way to help some students master the information and skills needed to meet high standards.

Of course, some school officials may still believe they are saving money by socially promoting students, so these administrators need to see how the resulting increases in spending on remedial services and special education referrals actually cost more and are less effective, thereby imperiling the administrators' jobs in two ways. And even at this late date, there may still be a few administrators who believe that "the research shows" additional learning and growing time does not provide "significant benefits." These administrators need to review a copy of *Real Facts from Real Schools*, by James Uphoff, Ed.D., which contains more than 50 research studies showing that additional time to learn and grow usually provides very real and important benefits, including improved academic performance.

Authoritative articles and books that convey this sort of information may be especially valuable, because they provide the documentation and reassurance the administrator may need in dealing with school board members, state education consultants, and other people in positions of authority. However, written texts should always be combined with invitations to visit classrooms and speak with students and their parents, so the administrators can see firsthand how and why a developmental approach is the best way to meet the educational needs of today's students.

From *Developmental Education in an Era of High Standards* by Jim Grant. Published by Modern Learning Press, Inc., P.O. Box 167, Rosemont, NJ 08556, 1-800-627-5867. This page may be reproduced by the individual purchaser only for his or her own use.

65

Q. How should parents and teachers participate in the development of standards for their schools?

A. It might appear obvious that teachers and parents should have a leading role in the development of standards for their schools, because teachers and parents have had the most firsthand experience with the children and therefore understand their real capabilities. Unfortunately, in many states the standards are being set by department of education bureaucrats with only token input from those who are most knowledgeable and will also be most affected by them.

This approach to developing standards is clearly inappropriate for a number of reasons. Perhaps most importantly, it effectively removes schools from local control, because the imposition of standards can and does have a drastic impact on the curriculum and methods of instruction used in many schools. And when state-level political appointees are in charge of setting educational standards, they are likely to be making decisions for political reasons, not just educational reasons, especially when governors and state legislators see education as a high-profile issue they can use to advance their personal agendas. In addition, it has been my experience that the people who have the least firsthand experience with a problem are usually the ones who are most certain they have the one and only solution to it.

Local control and site-based management are critical to the success of high standards. Standards should be developed by teachers and parents working with administrators and other members of the community, so that the standards accurately reflect where the students are now, what they are truly capable of achieving, and what is in the best interests of the students and the rest of the community. It may be possible, for example, to have many students score higher on a standardized test than they have in the past, but if many students also end up losing their enthusiasm for learning, engage in disruptive behavior, and develop negative attitudes about themselves, then the community needs to decide whether the accomplishment is truly worth the cost.

This process of setting incremental standards based on actual student performance, and then revising as needed, ensures that the standards will be child-compatible and effective. Unrealistic standards, on the other hand, are likely to have a corrupting effect on the curriculum and a frustrating effect on the students, all of which may then result in *less* actual learning and achievement. And, of course, it was *increased* learning and achievement that was supposed to result from establishing high standards in the first place.

Q. How can teachers and parents work together to help students achieve high standards?

A. There are numerous factors that contribute to successful achievement in school, and that's why high standards *alone* are not an effective means of improving achievement. Increased cooperation between teachers and parents is another important factor, and individually teachers and parents can help in other ways as well.

When teachers and parents present a "united front" in support of their specific school and its students, children are very likely to adapt a similar attitude and strive to perform and behave well. If, on the other hand, a parent or teacher presents a negative attitude about a specific individual or aspect of the education provided by a school, a young child is likely to start thinking in similar ways and act accordingly. And, in particular, if a parent and teacher are frequently at odds with each other, a young child may feel caught in the middle and start acting out in order to relieve the feelings of stress that the situation has created. This does not mean that either teachers or parents should refrain from talking about problems or disagreements with each other; it does mean that the discussions should be as constructive as possible and that conflict resolution techniques should be used if necessary.

To create a cooperative environment, teachers need to reach out to parents and recognize that this is a vitally important part of their job, even though teachers have not usually been trained to work with parents and may not receive much support for this work from administrators. Developmental educators must help parents feel welcome at the school and keep them informed about their children's progress, as well as any problems that may arise.

For their part, parents who want their children to meet high standards in school must also maintain high standards in their homes. To help students with their academic achievements, parents should read to and with their children regularly, and also demonstrate that they themselves read for information and enjoyment. Parents should also stay informed about homework and help when appropriate, and do their best to provide access to libraries. As much as possible, parents should also express support for the efforts made by their children, and try to provide the sort of stable, loving environment that helps children with their social, emotional, and physical development, as well as their intellectual development.

In ways such as this, the mutual efforts made by teachers and parents can reinforce one another, and enable students to achieve their full potential in school and in other aspects of their lives.

From *Developmental Education in an Era of High Standards* by Jim Grant. Published by Modern Learning Press, Inc., P.O. Box 167, Rosemont, NJ 08556, 1-800-627-5867. This page may be reproduced by the individual purchaser only for his or her own use.

Retention in an Era of High Standards

Q. What is retention and how can it help students?

A.

Retention is an educational intervention used to correct *wrong grade placement*—putting a child in a particular grade when the child is not yet ready to succeed in that grade. Retaining the child "in grade" for a second year provides the additional learning and growing time that some children need in order to *complete* the grade successfully, and then move up to the next grade level.

As discussed elsewhere in this book, there are three primary reasons that children end up being placed in the wrong grade. The main reason is that some children are *developmentally young* compared to other children of the same age. Developmentally young children can learn very successfully if given an additional year to develop in a supportive educational environment, but they are at great risk for failure if pressured to achieve and behave in ways that are virtually impossible for them at their current stage of development. A second reason is that the use of a single, arbitrary, and inflexible school entrance cut-off date results in a certain number of children being *chronologically younger* by almost a full year than the oldest students in a class, and this substantial disadvantage makes it far more difficult for many of the younger children to meet grade-level requirements. A third reason is that some children lack the prerequisite knowledge and skills to succeed in a grade due to their *personal backgrounds*, which may include an extended illness or simply a lack of exposure to basic information and skills. These children need additional time to learn what other children of the same age already know and are expected to know.

For any of these reasons, spending an additional year in the same grade may be the *only* way for a child to gain the knowledge and skills needed to complete the grade and meet high standards. When used in this way, retention is not a punishment or a judgment of the child; it is an adjustment and correction of inflexible regulations and difficult decisions made by educators and parents.

Decades of experience have shown that retention puts numerous children "back on track," by providing them with an opportunity to master material that they previously were unable to handle. These children then feel good about themselves as students and as individuals because they know that they can and do learn successfully, rather than continually struggling and failing, and then feeling "dumb," inadequate, and resentful as a result.

Of course, there are some children for whom retention is *not* appropriate. And there are many children for whom retention *alone* is not enough, because they need other interventions along with additional learning and growing time. Educators and parents therefore have a responsibility to make informed decisions about children's initial grade placement and the use of time-flexibility options such as retention.

From *Developmental Education in an Era of High Standards* by Jim Grant. Published by Modern Learning Press, Inc., P.O. Box 167, Rosemont, NJ 08556, 1-800-627-5867. This page may be reproduced by the individual purchaser only for his or her own use.

Q. What types of children are likely to benefit from retention, and what types of children are not?

A. As noted on the previous page, retention is primarily an intervention for children who have been placed in the wrong grade because they are developmentally young, chronologically young, or have a deficit of knowledge and skills due to their personal backgrounds. Beyond that, however, there are other factors and circumstances that educators and parents should consider when making decisions about the retention of a child.

Children are *most* likely to benefit from retention when the need for additional learning and growing time is the only problem they face, and when they and their parents all support the decision to spend an additional year completing a grade. Retention is also more likely to be successful if the children are average or above in ability, so they are fully capable of doing the required work, and if they are relatively small for their age, so they are likely to fit in better with younger children.

Children are *least* likely to benefit from retention when they are suffering from a variety of complex problems that retention may further exacerbate, and when they and their parents oppose retention. If the children are unmotivated due to depression or some other emotional problem, or if they have a serious and recurrent behavior or conduct disorder, they are also unlikely to use an additional year in the same grade to learn and achieve successfully. And if children have *already* received an additional year of learning and growing time, and so are already one year older than the other students in a grade, they should *not* be given a second year because the age difference will be too great and probably lead to other problems in the later grades.

Essentially, then, the key considerations are whether retention is the appropriate intervention for the student's problem, and whether the student will be able to use the additional learning and growing time to gain needed information and skills. Obviously, this requires educators and parents to make decisions on an individual basis. If, for example, a child fits all the criteria for benefiting from an additional year, but the child and the child's parents are vehemently opposed to retention, I believe the intervention should not be used because it is almost destined to fail.

A final consideration is whether the child will also receive all other needed interventions. In some locations, a child may be denied other services simply because the child is receiving an additional year of school. This not only makes retention more likely to fail, it is also morally wrong and potentially illegal. Retention should *not* be a substitute for any other educational intervention—it should be used to help children who have specific types of problems, and, if necessary, used in conjunction with other interventions.

Q. When is the best time for a child to be retained?

A. The best time is the same year that the educators and parents first decide that the child is likely to benefit from an additional year of growing and learning time. Retention is an intervention designed to alleviate serious problems that a child is having in school, and when the problems are allowed to continue, children tend to fall even further behind and develop even poorer habits and attitudes.

Each successive year that a child fails to learn needed information and skills makes it even more difficult for the child to catch up and succeed in the following grades. As explained in the booklet *Starting School*, by veteran kindergarten teacher Judy Keshner, *"Each grade builds on the one that came before, and kindergarten sets the pattern and the tone...When children face a school environment that is too busy for their current stage of development, they start to see themselves as incapable of doing anything right. This is where the pattern of failure begins, and it may never go away."*

My own experience and that of many other educators has been that school failure is cumulative and increases in momentum as its duration lengthens. Implementing a retention decision as soon as possible interrupts this process by preventing bad study habits and inappropriate behaviors from being reinforced while the child's confidence and self-esteem are also being badly damaged. Instead, a child who has additional learning and growing time can gain needed information and skills, and do better in comparison both to other students and to his or her own previous performance, thereby developing a better self-image and attitude about school.

Another advantage of intervention in the early primary grades is that student groupings are usually less distinct and less important to young children, who are more likely to be concerned about their own experiences than what a few other students may think of them. When a child has risen through the grades with the same classmates for several years and then "stays back," the adjustment can be much more difficult, although ultimately still worthwhile.

Some school systems have prohibited retention before third or fourth grade, supposedly to "protect" young students. But by allowing the quantities of children in need of additional learning time to increase from year to year, along with the extent of the children's problems, administrators have then found that an overly large percentage of the student population is in need of retention when they reach the minimum grade level. And retention alone is then less effective academically and financially because the children's problems may now require additional interventions, as well.

In contrast, many parents who eventually allowed their child to have an additional year of learning and growing time told me later, "If we had only known, we would have done it much sooner."

Q. What alternatives to retention should also be considered?

A. Essentially, there are two true alternatives to retention—*transition* and *multiage* classes—which can work for *every* child who needs an additional year of learning and growing time. There are also some other, more limited options that may work for *some* children who need additional time.

Transition classes allow children to continue their progress in a year-long class between two standard grades, such as kindergarten and first grade. This enables the students to keep on developing the knowledge, skills, and maturity needed to succeed in the grade that follows, but to do so in a new classroom with a new curriculum and a new teacher. Multiage classes combine children of different ages, such as 5- to 8-year-olds. The range of age levels and developmental stages in these classes make them a comfortable place for some children to spend an additional year.

Other options provide a limited amount of additional time, but not the full year of school that some children need. For example, a number of schools now offer or require *summer school* sessions for children who need to make further progress in order to succeed at the next grade level. This can help students who are just a few months behind in their work, but not those who have more serious knowledge deficits or who need far more time to mature. In a similar way, *remediation* and after-school *tutoring* can also provide more "time on task," as well as the individualized instruction that can make a big difference for some—but not all—students.

Some promoters of specialized *reading programs* claim that these programs are an effective alternative to retention, which may be true in situations where a child may be retained *solely* because of a reading problem. However, most failing students have problems in a number of subject areas, and one of the best-known reading programs can only be used with first graders who have *not* had an additional year of learning time, and whose records do *not* show high absenteeism, frequent changes of address, learning disabilities, or other circumstances often identified with failure.

There are also still some promoters of "developmentally appropriate practices" who claim that their approach to education will enable all children to "catch up" in third grade, thereby eliminating the need for retention. However, I know of not even *one* elementary school anywhere in America where this has actually occurred. This lack of success has virtually eliminated interest in this so-called alternative.

Finally, for some students who are not likely or able to benefit from retention, the only alternative may be *social promotion*, which means they will probably be promoted year after year without having learned needed information and skills. Some of these students may find the help they need, or achieve breakthroughs for other reasons, but many face bleak prospects in school and beyond.

Q. How should decisions about retention be made?

A. Parents should make the final decision about retaining a child, based on information and advice provided by the child's teacher, principal, and other members of the school staff.

During the first few weeks of the school year, many experienced teachers can recognize children who have been placed in the wrong grade and who would benefit from an additional year to learn and complete the curriculum. In other cases, new problems may emerge during the year and prevent the child from learning the information and skills needed to succeed at the next grade level. Either way, as soon as a teacher thinks that a child is at risk, immediate action should be taken.

The child's teacher should alert other educators and administrators, as well as the child's parents, while still doing everything possible to help the child catch up and succeed. Often, a "child study team" comprised of the teacher, an administrator, and relevant specialists will evaluate the child's current situation and develop an intervention plan. Parental input should also be solicited, and the parents should be encouraged to provide intensified academic and emotional support for their child.

The teacher should continue to document the child's problems, progress, all the steps taken to provide individualized assistance to the child, and communications with the parents and relevant members of the school staff. By the late winter or early spring, all the people involved should be well aware of the child's current status, what steps have been taken, and where the child needs to be in order to be ready to succeed at the next grade level. The teacher and child study team can then prepare a recommendation to be presented to the parents in an informal meeting.

At the meeting, the teacher should clarify that the purpose of the meeting is to discuss ways to help the child, and that the parents' input will be important. The teacher should discuss and document the information described above, explain the recommendation being made, ask for an initial reaction from the parents, and then advise them to consider and discuss the information further before making a final decision. Obviously, the child should also be consulted by the parents, and if at all possible, the parents should be referred to other parents who are willing to discuss their own experiences in giving or refusing their child an additional year of learning time.

When a retention decision is handled this way, the parents, educators, and students involved often reach a unanimous agreement that taking an additional year to complete the curriculum is the best approach. While school officials can retain a child without parental approval, this is *not* likely to be a positive and successful experience for the child, so I do not recommend it.

Q. What should happen after the decision is made to retain a child?

A. Essentially, educators and parents must then work together to formulate plans for successful academic intervention and for effective communication with the key participants.

In addition to deciding whether to retain a child, the educators and parents must also decide *how* to retain the child. If the child and current teacher work well together, keeping the child with the teacher for another year may make the most sense, because it will save them time getting to know one another, and it can make better use of the existing supportive relationship. Otherwise, it may be preferable for the child to spend the second year with a new teacher at the same school, with a new teacher at a new school, or, if possible and appropriate, with a parent capable of "home schooling" the child for a year.

Whatever type of retention is used, the educators and parents involved should agree on a detailed plan for meeting the academic, social, and emotional needs of the child. Just as students who have disabilities are supposed to have an Individual Education Plan prepared for them, when students are retained there should be an Individual Retention Plan that outlines the strategies and techniques that will be used to help the students reach specific academic and behavioral goals. This plan should be reviewed periodically to determine how the student is progressing and whether any changes or additional interventions are needed.

A vitally important part of the process is the way in which parents discuss the retention decision with their child. Certainly, it should not come as a surprise to the child, who should have been involved in discussions about his or her academic problems and potential solutions throughout the year. This discussion should come as a natural and logical outgrowth of these previous discussions, and it should include a review of those discussions and of the efforts made by the child and others to improve the child's academic performance. Most of all, this should be a true *two-way* conversation, with ample opportunity for the child to talk about his or her academic, social, and emotional experiences during the year.

I recommend acknowledging the child's intelligence and efforts, and explaining that the child probably needs more time to learn and grow in order to complete the work for this grade and move on to the next grade successfully. Then, a parent can say something such as, "That's why we and your teacher would like you spend another year in this grade, and we want to know how you feel about that." Not only does this approach help the child become an active participant in the conversation, it may also provide some unexpected and valuable information, such as the fact that the child is *relieved* rather than upset about the decision.

Q. Doesn't research show that retention is bad for children?

A. No, the most comprehensive, convincing, and recent research shows that retention can and does help some children, but not all children. To say that *all* the research leads to just one conclusion would be as simplistic and unrealistic as saying that retention is right for all children, or that it is wrong for all children.

Recent and ongoing studies conducted by researchers at the prestigious Johns Hopkins University confirm that retention helps a significant number of students. And this research confirms that some of the negative outcomes linked by critics to retention are actually due to other factors. As Johns Hopkins researcher Doris Entwistle explained in the December 4th, 1996 issue of *Education Week*, "*We know, because we have data from when these children began school, that the ones who are held back in 1st grade have terrible problems to start with…And so, later on, when children who have been retained do not do well, all of that deficit in performance cannot be attributed to the fact that they've been held back.*"

This point might seem so obvious as to not even be worth noting, but it has apparently eluded some of the critics who continue to insist that retention alone is responsible for the later troubles of children who were struggling and failing long before they were retained, and who may also have had documented social and emotional problems before they even started school. Of course, it should probably come as no surprise that some of the most outspoken critics of additional learning time are university professors who have done their own research studies, which just happen to confirm their point of view and are widely cited by their fellow critics. Meanwhile, other studies that document the benefits of retention are totally ignored by them.

As mentioned elsewhere in this book and documented in *Real Facts from Real Schools*, by James Uphoff, Ed.D., all methods of providing students with an additional year of learning time were subjected to an extensive negative media campaign during the late 1980s and early 1990s. The organizers of this campaign continually cited the same small group of professors as the source of the information used to attack retention and transition classes, while promoting the use of "developmentally appropriate practices" as an alternative to additional learning time. Now that these practices have *not* been found to be an effective substitution for learning time, the campaign has died down, but much of the research remains in circulation.

Educators and parents therefore need to make sure they review the full range of research about this topic and maintain a healthy skepticism about it all, rather than falling for self-serving claims and statistical manipulations of a few professors who have their own agendas and priorities. Then, and most of all, educators and parents need to pay attention to the individual children and school under consideration.

Q. How should retention be used in an era of high standards?

A. Retention should be used as an academic intervention that helps some struggling students learn successfully and meet high standards. Ultimately, this can be done in one of two ways.

Retention works best when it is used as a form of *early* intervention to help a child who has started having serious difficulties and falling behind, but who has not yet developed the bad habits and negative attitudes that accompany years of daily failure in school. An additional year of growing and learning time at an early age has helped many struggling students become successful and confident learners.

Retention can also help older students who need and want an additional year to complete a grade successfully. In many cases, older students who were retained have found that for the first time in all their years of school, they were capable of learning and achieving like their classmates, and this experience then had a very positive effect on their self-image, as well as on their report cards.

Of course, there are also ways in which retention should *not* be used during an era of high standards. First and foremost, I do not believe retention should be used as a threat or punishment. Children start out wanting to learn, and those who become continually struggling and failing students need appropriate help and support. They also need to experience limits and consequences, but an additional year of learning and growing time is too expensive and precious to waste on students who cannot or will not benefit from it. Also, portraying retention as a negative experience is very likely to make it a less effective and desirable intervention for the students who really do need it and want it.

In addition, retention should *not* be used as an automatic consequence of a low score on a standardized test. Responsible educators and parents need to consider a variety of factors and then make an informed decision about each individual student, if a year of the child's life and the corresponding budget allocation are to be well spent.

Finally, retention should *not* be used as a political bandwagon whose real purpose is to transport an ambitious politician to a higher office. Some politicians have tried to prove that they're as "tough" on school failure as they are on crime, even though failing students are far more likely to be victims than perpetrators. These politicians' rhetoric and proposals are not only likely to prove counter-productive in schools, they are also likely to prove counter-productive in the political arena, where the decency and common sense of most American voters enable them to spot the difference between mean-spirited bullies and effective leaders. The education of our children can and should be a political issue, but politicians must handle it as seriously and responsibly as the educators and parents directly involved.

School Reform
in an Era of
High Standards

Q. Does the history of recent school reforms have anything to teach us about the current emphasis on standards?

A. Yes. In recent decades there has been a consistent pattern of "pendulum swings," in which one type of reform is taken to an extreme and then results in a counter-reform that goes too far in the opposite direction. This pattern leads to ineffective reforms that do not make sense, do not last, and hurt students and their schools, while also generating widespread cynicism about the school reform process and the entire American public school system.

Prime examples of this trend include the switch from phonics to an ineffective form of whole language, the switch from developmental education to an unrealistic version of "developmentally appropriate practices," the switch from special education to full inclusion regardless of students' needs, and the switch from selective retention to mandatory social promotion for all students. All of these changes initially grew out of valid insights but were taken by some proponents to such an illogical extreme that they prevented educators from doing their jobs well, and then ultimately led to a backlash. Specifically, the extreme versions of whole language, developmentally appropriate practice, full inclusion, and social promotion prevented many teachers from providing effective skills instruction to the full range of students in their classes.

Another important characteristic of this pattern is that the extreme positions tend to be taken and promoted by "reformers" who do not actually work with children on a regular basis. University professors, state and association bureaucrats, financially motivated publishers, politicians, and other people *not* directly involved in the education of children have often been in the forefront of efforts to establish their approach as the one and only answer for *all* children, effectively *prohibiting* educators from taking more moderate and balanced positions. This top-down, ideological approach often succeeds in gaining media attention and forcing teachers to do what they're told initially, but then as the ineffectiveness and outright harm of the extreme position become apparent to educators and parents directly involved with real children, support falters and disappears.

This pattern is far less likely to occur with a bottom-up reform process, in which a grass-roots movement of educators and parents—who are directly involved with students—identifies and then helps to spread an effective solution. This is what happened when developmental education first became popular during the late 1960s. Parents and educators tend to rely more on common sense, reason, local choice, and multiple approaches, because these adults have direct interactions with children and recognize the many complexities and exceptions that prevent a single, exclusive ideological position from being as valid as its proponents claim.

Q. How does the current emphasis on standards fit into the pattern of school-reform pendulum swings?

A. Unfortunately, the enthusiasm for standards has already shown signs of going too far, raising the possibility that it will become one more *failed* effort at school reform, because extremists who do not actually work with children are focusing more on the standards than on the children the standards are supposed to help.

Like other failed efforts at school reform, the standards movement started out as a logical and even predictable reaction to previous failed efforts at school reform. In this case, the need to establish grade-level standards became apparent as extreme proponents of whole language and developmentally appropriate practices prevented students from learning needed skills, and then extreme proponents of social promotion insisted that the students be promoted every year even when they lacked basic knowledge and skills. Under these circumstances, reasonable standards were an effective way of making sure that teachers taught and students learned what was needed.

In several cases, however, establishing standards became a means for some politicians and bureaucrats to establish how "tough" they were, and for some education officials to show that their students could learn more than other students could. The extreme standards that resulted were way out of line with what many students could and should achieve, which put pressure on the students and their teachers to focus on meeting inappropriate standards rather than on gaining important knowledge and skills. A further result is likely to be the poor performance and negative attitudes that occur when students are pressured to exceed their natural capabilities.

Another similarity with past failed reforms is that the enthusiasm for standards is resulting in a headlong rush to implement a new approach without having shown that it actually does any good. Just as proponents claimed that developmentally appropriate practices would eliminate the need for additional learning time, even though this was *never* shown to occur at even one elementary school anywhere in America, the standards bandwagon has set off at a rapid pace without valid studies showing that it will actually help the full range of students at real American schools. Rather than a proven solution, then, the establishment of high standards is actually an experiment that is using millions of American students as guinea pigs.

There is good reason to believe that the establishment of appropriate standards will improve the performance of our students and schools. On that basis, and knowing that America's children have been failed by several recent attempts at school reform, we have a responsibility to proceed in a moderate and cautious way. Educators, reformers, and standard setters, like doctors, should be required to follow the same basic principle: *First, do no harm.*

Q.

What other aspects of education should also be given a high priority at this time?

A.

As noted earlier, extreme proponents of high standards for students seem far less eager to establish high standards for students' childhoods or even their basic needs—such as nutrition, health care, and shelter—which clearly affect a child's ability to learn and perform well in school. And it may come as no surprise that extreme proponents of high standards for students also seem far less eager to establish high standards for other aspects of the educational experience that is supposed to enable students to succeed.

Take, for example, the issue of funding for education. Students in a suburban district often receive far more funding per pupil than students in a nearby inner city district. And while money alone is not a solution, it is certainly a factor. When one group of students has higher-quality materials, smaller class sizes, and more access to support personnel, it should be and usually is easier for them to meet high standards. So, one way to help *all* American students meet high standards is to establish high (and fair) standards for educational funding.

High standards are also needed in regard to children's readiness to succeed in school. As noted earlier in this book, school readiness stems from good nutrition, comprehensive health care, effective parenting, and other basic needs of a child. It is also related to high-quality preschool and other early experiences that provide children with the information and social/emotional skills they need to succeed. And it is related to school entrance policies that enable all children to become eligible to start kindergarten at the same age, rather than requiring children in some states or districts to start learning the same material and meeting the same standards when they are significantly younger than children in neighboring areas.

High standards are also needed in regard to mandates and attempts at education reform. Teachers and students need to be *protected* from politically and commercially driven programs that have not been proven to work in America's public schools, unless the teachers and parents all *volunteer* to participate in the experiment and have the children in their care serve as guinea pigs. Too often, teachers are ordered to carry out programs that are likely to fail, and then blamed when the programs and the students involved do fail. Students and their schools cannot be expected to meet high standards under these circumstances.

Obviously, there is less resistance to establishing high standards for children than to establishing high standards for voters, taxpayers, corporations, and political parties. Perhaps establishing high standards for the latter people and organizations should come first, as that would probably enable more students to meet high standards.

Q. What role should politics have in education reform at this time?

A. Many elected officials have made positive contributions to education reform in recent years, and as long as the politicians represent the best interests of America's children along with their other constituents, they can and should remain important participants in the education reform process.

A prime example of their positive influence is the stand against social promotion taken by many local and national politicians. To a large extent, they have succeeded in expressing the will of the people and stopping policies that prevented many children from receiving the additional learning time and full education the children needed and deserved. The ongoing interest in establishing high standards and helping students meet them is also valuable, but now politicians need to complete the process by acknowledging that some new standards are inappropriate for America's children, and then hold the standards' creators accountable for the damage they have done.

Now that education reform has become a hot political issue, it is also vulnerable to some of the same unfortunate tendencies that affect other aspects of the political process. Demagogues may try to use education reform to increase their own power, misinformation and disinformation may be spread by politically motivated groups that believe their ends justify any means, people and businesses may try to diminish or divert the large sums of tax dollars involved, and so on.

In particular, and as noted elsewhere in this book, the emphasis on standards has revealed a very negative aspect of politicians' involvement in the education reform process. Some politicians have tried to prove their "toughness" by promoting inappropriate standards along with related policies that are also harmful, such as automatic retention for students who do not achieve a specific score on one standardized test. Because children do not vote or have political action committees that can funnel money to legislators, it is all too easy for some irresponsible politicians to ignore the real educational needs of America's children.

That leaves America's parents and teachers responsible for monitoring politicians' involvement in education reform. When politicians work effectively with parents and teachers to improve students' education, they need and deserve intense support from parents and teachers. When politicians use students' education to further their own ambitions, they need and deserve to be removed from office as quickly as possible. That's how our political system works, and concerned adults must at least *try* to make it work for our children.

Q. What role should businesses have in education reform?

A. Like politics, businesses can have a positive influence on education reform, but they can also interfere with the process and distort it.

Businesses that enter into partnerships with schools, providing tutors, training, feedback about needed skills, and other forms of support, provide a great role model of responsible citizenship. In a less direct way, businesses have also shown how education administrators can manage and spend their funds more effectively, and how streamlining bureaucracies can sometimes make them more efficient, rather than less capable. And businesses have also demonstrated how a commitment to customer service and willingness to listen to all the "stakeholders" in an organization can make it work better for everyone involved.

On the other hand, some businesses that are solely focused on their profitability may feel it is reasonable or even obligatory to oppose needed funding for schools, because those funds would sustain or increase taxes on the business but not provide any immediate benefits to it. Businesses that rely on students to provide part-time help may end up pressuring students to work longer than is good for them and their school work. And some businesses may be reluctant to provide needed child-care services or allow parents to take time needed to provide intellectual or emotional support for their children.

As will be discussed further on the following page, some businesses are now trying to make money on students by setting up for-profit elementary schools. Unlike traditional private and religious schools, the ultimate purpose of these schools is to turn a profit, and in some cases these businesses even have stock that is publicly traded, so they are subject to pressure from shareholders who may want ever-greater profitability. While there is *some* validity to the standard refrain that the businesses will only make long-term profits if they do a good job, the reality is that some businesses make money in the short term by doing a lousy job, and some businesses fail so completely they go out of business altogether, leaving their customers in the lurch. I believe the primary purpose of a school should always be to provide the best possible education for its students, so there is an inherent conflict of interest when profitability is also a top priority.

One of the strengths of America's business community has been that it fiercely resists outside interference from government officials and others who try to interfere with its operations. Committed educators and parents may have something to learn from the business community in this regard, as they focus on providing American children with the schools they truly need and deserve.

Q.

What role should charter schools and vouchers have in education reform?

A.

Charter schools and vouchers pose very different issues, but taken together they provide a good basis for comparing and contrasting their effects.

Charter schools have piqued the interest of educators and parents, who in many cases have shown how much can be accomplished when they are freed from bureaucratic red tape and can then work together on realistic reforms. High-quality charter schools have shown they can provide a very valuable educational experience for their students, in addition to serving as an important model for other schools.

Unfortunately, a few charter schools have been a disaster for students, as ineptitude and mismanagement resulted in the schools disintegrating and failing during the school year. Other schools have stayed open but delivered far less than their elaborate and overly enticing sales pitches promised, using some untrained and inexperienced personnel to provide an inappropriate and ineffective curriculum. To make matters worse, in some states these sorts of charter schools actually divert money from public schools, thereby hurting the students left behind in public school, as well as the students trapped in the failing or ineffective schools.

Unlike charter schools, vouchers are *not* something I can support. While vouchers are sometimes promoted as a way to help poor children attend better schools, many of those students are likely to be rejected by the private schools they would like to attend. Even the lucky few who are accepted are likely to find that the vouchers will not cover all the needed expenses, imposing a severe financial hardship on family members, as well as creating social and emotional pressures.

Most of all, vouchers directly divert funds from public schools to private schools, which are not only free to reject students for any reason at all, but can also indoctrinate accepted students with viewpoints and beliefs that are not supported by a majority of local taxpayers. I strongly support America's public schools precisely because they are committed to educating *all* of America's children, however difficult that may prove, and because they are governed by *elected* school board members and other officials, who can be voted out of office or have their budgets cut. Vouchers, in contrast, can end up supporting exclusivity and the diversion of public funds to people who may not be accountable to voters or taxpayers.

Obviously, there are many high-quality charter, private, and religious schools that provide a very good education to the students they accept. They remain an important alternative in our society, but high-quality public schools are an absolute necessity for all types of children and should not have needed funds diverted from them.

Q. What role should new technologies have in education reform?

A. As with so many other aspects of education reform, new technologies have the potential to enhance student learning and achievement, but organizations promoting them can and do over-sell their capabilities and benefits.

Computers are a prime example. They can clearly stimulate interest in subject areas and provide a means of researching them. They can also prove helpful in the editing and "publishing" of student work as part of process writing. And some teachers have found that certain software helps their students practice basic skills.

Obviously, the preceding, carefully qualified statements are far less enthusiastic than the glowing pronouncements made by computer companies and their supporters. For while familiarity with and access to computers is becoming a basic element of education and career training, many educators have been very disappointed with the software supposedly designed to teach students such things as reading and writing. And to the extent that computers are used as a substitute for human contact and a truly individualized curriculum, they can have a very negative impact on students, rather than just being ineffective.

In fact, computers are the latest in a long line of new technologies that were supposed to "revolutionize" teaching. As David Elkind points out in *Reinventing Childhood*, early in the 20th century predictions were being made that movies and radios would replace textbooks and blackboards. While these technologies and others were found to have some educational value, (human) teachers and books remain the key elements of education, and this is not likely to change any time soon.

One change that has occurred, and not necessarily for the better, is that television and videos now have a regular place in many classrooms. Television programs and videos may have educational merit, if used in context with other forms of learning and accompanied by appropriate discussion, but these media may also reinforce the passivity and other bad habits that many young children learn all too well at home. In particular, the use of TV and videos in schools can be a form of "hurrying" the development of children in an unhealthy way, in that it may assume a level of media sophistication that does not actually exist, thereby exposing children to images and messages that they are not yet ready to comprehend and interpret. This is especially true when children are required to sit through televised advertisements in the classroom, because their schools have been enticed by the lure of free equipment to expose their students to marketers of youth-oriented products.

Effective education requires active investigation and coordination with other people. New technologies enhance some aspects of this process, but they can never replace it.

Q. Is the education reform process proceeding in the right way?

A. No. As indicated throughout this chapter, now that education reform has become a hot political issue and a potential source of revenue for big business, in many cases it is being influenced by agendas and policies that serve the needs of people other than the students themselves. In addition, too many of the latest education reforms have repeated past mistakes by going to extremes and skipping important steps, such as gathering detailed input from teachers and parents, building a consensus, and using firsthand research from local schools as a basis for initial decisions and ongoing review.

After all the failed reforms and pendulum swings and damage done to American students, the real basis for effective education reform should no longer be a mystery that requires further trial-and-error learning. Education reform needs to be a grassroots process led by educators and parents who have firsthand experience with today's children, and who will still be around when the results of their efforts become apparent. The process also needs to be moderate, gradual, based on common sense, confirmed by research, and driven by a genuine concern for children.

If this approach to education reform sounds similar to the developmental approach to education described elsewhere in this book, it should. Like the children they serve, schools also need concerned grown-ups to demonstrate understanding, support, and an awareness of their differing needs and capabilities, as well as a commitment to helping them meet high standards.

Bibliography

Albert, Linda. *An Administrator's Guide to Cooperative Discipline*. Circle Pines, MN: American Guidance, 1989.

Albert, Linda. *Cooperative Discipline: How to Manage Your Classroom and Promote Self-Esteem*. Circle Pines, MN: American Guidance, 1996.

Alexander, Karl; Entwistle, Doris and Dauber, Susan L. *On the Success of Failure: A Reassessment of the Effects of Retention in the Primary Grades*, Cambridge, England: Cambridge University Pres, 1994.

Ames, Louise Bates. *What Am I Doing In This Grade?* Rosemont, NJ: Modern Learning Press, 1985.

Ames, Louise Bates. *Your Four-Year-Old: Wild and Wonderful*. New York: Dell, 1980.

Ames, Louise Bates. *Your Five-Year-Old: Sunny and Serene*. New York: Dell, 1979.

Ames, Louise Bates. *Your Six-Year-Old: Defiant but Loving*. New York: Dell, 1979.

Ames, Louise Bates. *Your Seven-Year-Old: Life in a Minor Key*. New York: Dell, 1985.

Ames, Louise Bates. *Your Eight-Year-Old: Lively and Outgoing*. New York: Dell, 1989.

Ames, Louise Bates. *Your Nine-Year-Old: Thoughtful and Mysterious*. New York: Dell, 1990.

Boyer, Ernest. *Ready to Learn: A Mandate for the Nation*. Princeton, NJ: The Foundation for the Advancement of Teaching, 1991.

Brazelton, T. Berry. *Touchpoints: The Essential Reference. Your Child's Emotional and Behavioral Development*. Reading, MA: Addison-Wesley, 1994.

Coletta, Anthony. *Kindergarten Readiness Checklist for Parents*. Rosemont, NJ: Modern Learning Press, 1991.

Coletta, Anthony. *What's Best for Kids: A Guide to Developmentally Appropriate Practices for Teachers & Parents of Children Ages 4-8*. Rosemont, NJ: Modern Learning Press, 1991.

Elkind, David. *Parenting Your Teenager*. New York:Ballantine, 1994.

Elkind, David. *Reinventing Childhood*. Rosemont, NJ: Modern Learning Press, 1998.

Elkind, David. *The Hurried Child*. Reading, MA: Addison-Wesley, 1981.

Elovson, Allanna. *The Kindergarten Survival Book*. Santa Monica, CA: Parent Ed Resources, 1991.

From *Developmental Education in an Era of High Standards* by Jim Grant. Published by Modern Learning Press, Inc., P.O. Box 167, Rosemont, NJ 08556, 1-800-627-5867. This page may be reproduced by the individual purchaser only for his or her own use.

91

Fassler, David G. and Dumas, Lynne S. *"Help Me, I'm Sad"*. New York, NY: Penguain Putnam, Inc., 1997.

Forsten, Char. *The Multiyear Lesson Plan Book*. Peterborough, NH: Crystal Springs Books, 1996.

Forsten, Char; Grant, Jim; Johnson, Bob and Richardson, Irv. *Looping Q & A*, Peterborough, NH: Crystal Springs Books, 1997.

Goodman, Gretchen. *I Can Learn*, Peterborough, NH: Crystal Springs Books, 1995.

Goodman, Gretchen. *More I Can Learn*, Peterborough, NH: Crystal Springs Books, 1998.

Grant, Jim and Johnson, Bob. *A Common Sense Guide to Multiage Practices*. Columbus, OH: Teachers' Publishing Group, 1995.

Grant, Jim. *Do You Know Where Your Child Is?* Video. Rosemont, NJ: Modern Learning Press, 1985.

Grant, Jim and Azen, Margot. *Every Parent's Owner's Manuals. (Three-, Four-, Five-, Six-, Seven-Year-Old)*. Rosemont, NJ: Modern Learning Press.

Grant, Jim and Johnson, Bob. *First Grade Readiness Checklist*. Peterborough, NH: Society For Developmental Education, 1997.

Grant, Jim. *"I Hate School!" Some Common-Sense Answers For Educators & Parents Who Want To Know Why & What To Do About It*. Rosemont, NJ: Modern Learning Press, 1994.

Grant, Jim and Johnson, Bob. *Kindergarten Readiness Checklist*. Peterborough, NH: Society For Developmental Education, 1997.

Grant, Jim; Johnson, Bob; and Richardson, Irv. *The Looping Handbook: Teachers and Students Progressing Together*. Peterborough, NH: Crystal Springs Books, 1996.

Grant, Jim; Johnson, Bob; and Richardson, Irv. *Multiage Q & A: 101 Practical Answers to Your Most Pressing Questions*. Peterborough, NH: Crystal Springs Books, 1995.

Grant, Jim; Johnson, Bob; and Richardson, Irv. *Our Best Advice: The Multiage Problem Solving Handbook*. Peterborough, NH: Crystal Springs Books, 1996.

Grant, Jim. *Retention & Its Prevention*. Rosemont, NJ: Modern Learning Press, 1997.

Grant, Jim and Richardson, Irv. *The Retention/Promotion Checklist*, Peterborough, NH: Crystal Springs Books, 1998.

Hallowell, Edward M., and Ratey, John J. *Driven to Distraction*. New York: Touchstone, 1994.

Healy, Jane M. *Endangered Minds: Why Children Don't Think and What We Can Do About It*. New York: Simon and Schuster, 1990.

Healy, Jane M. *Your Child's Growing Mind: A Guide to Learning and Brain Development From Birth to Adolescence*. New York: Doubleday, 1987.

Healy, Jane M. and Healy, Jane A. *Failure To Connect: How Computers Affect Our Children's Minds - For Better And Worse*, New York, NY: Simon & Schuster, 1998.

Hobby, Janice Hale. *Staying Back*. Gainesville, FL: Triad, 1990.

Hoffman, Carol. *Reaching & Teaching The Kids Today*. Rosemont, NJ: Modern Learning Press, 1996.

Keshner, Judy. *The Kindergarten Teacher's Very Own Student Observation & Assessment Guide*. Rosemont, NJ: Modern Learning Press, 1996.

Keshner, Judy. *Starting School: A Parent's Guide to the Kindergarten Year*. Rosemont, NJ: Modern Learning Press, 1990.

Kotulak, Ronald. *Inside the Brain*, Kansas City, MO: Andrews McMeel Publishing, 1996.

Lamb, Beth, and Logsdon, Phyllis. *Positively Kindergarten: A Classroom-proven, Theme-based, Developmental Guide for the Kindergarten Teacher*. Rosemont, NJ: Modern Learning Press, 1991.

National Education Commission on Time and Learning. *Prisoners of Time*. Washington, DC: U.S. Government Printing Office, Superintendent of Documents, 1994.

Uphoff, James K. *Real Facts From Real Schools: What You're Not Supposed To Know About School Readiness and Transition Programs*. Rosemont, NJ: Modern Learning Press, 1990, 1995.

Uphoff, James K.; Gilmore, June E. and Huber, Rosemarie. *Summer Children: Ready Or Not For School*, Middletown, Ohio: J & J Publishing, 1987.

Vail, Priscilla. *Emotion: The On-Off Switch for Learning*. Rosemont, NJ: Modern Learning Press, 1994.

Wood, Chip. *Yardsticks: Children in the Classroom Ages 4-14*. Greenfield, MA: Northeast Foundation for Children, 1994.

Other Great Books Available From
Modern Learning Press

Retention & Its Prevention
by Jim Grant

"I Hate School!"
by Jim Grant

Reinventing Childhood
by David Elkind

Real Facts From Real Schools
by James Uphoff

For more information, contact
Modern Learning Press, Inc.
P.O. Box 167
Rosemont, NJ 08556

or call toll-free
1-800-627-5867